The EFQM Excellence Model
For Assessing Organizational Performance
A Management Guide

Other publications by Van Haren Publishing

Van Haren Publishing specializes in titles on Best Practices, methods and standards within IT and business management.
These publications are grouped in the following series: ITSM Library (on behalf of ITSMF International), *Best Practice* and *IT Management Topics*.
At the time of going to press the following books are available:

ITIL
Foundations of IT Service Management based on ITIL®, (English, Dutch, French, German, Spanish, Japanese, Chinese, Danish, Italian, Korean, Russian, Arabic; also available as a CD-ROM)
Implementing Service and Support Management Processes (English)
IT Service Management - een samenvatting, 2de druk (Dutch)
IT Service Management - een leerboek (Dutch)
Release and Control for IT Service Management, based on ITIL® - A Practitioner Guide (English)

ISO/IEC 20000
ISO/IEC 20000 - A Pocket Guide (English, Italian, German, Spanish, Portuguese)

ISO 27001 and ISO 17799
Information Security based on ISO 27001 and ISO 17799 - A Management Guide (English)
Implementing Information Security based on ISO 27001 and ISO 17799 - A Management Guide (English)

CobiT
IT Governance based on CobiT4® - A Management Guide (English, German)

IT Service CMM
IT Service CMM - A Pocket Guide (English)

ASL
ASL - A Framework for Application Management (English)
ASL - Application Services Library - A Management Guide (English, Dutch)

BiSL
BiSL - A Framework for Business Information Management (Dutch; English)
BiSL - Business information Services Library - A Management Guide (Dutch; English edition due Summer 2007)

ISPL
IT Services Procurement op basis van ISPL (Dutch)
IT Services Procurement based on ISPL – A Pocket Guide (English)

ISO 9000
ISO 9001:2000 - The Quality Management Process (English)

EFQM
The EFQM Excellence Model For Assessing Organizational Performance – A Management Guide (English)

PRINCE2
Project Management based on PRINCE2™- Edition 2005 (English, Dutch, German)
PRINCE2™ - A No Nonsense Management Guide (English)
PRINCE2™ voor opdrachtgevers – Management Guide (Dutch)

MSP
Programme Management based on MSP (English, Dutch)
Programme Management based on MSP - A Management Guide (English)

M_o_R
Risk Management based on M_o_R - A Management Guide (English)

Topics & Management instruments
De RfP voor IT-outsourcing (Dutch; English version due summer 2007)
Decision- en Controlfactoren voor IT-Sourcing (Dutch)
Defining IT Success through the Service Catalog (English)
Frameworks for IT Management - An introduction (English; German edition due Autumn 2007)
Implementing leading standards for IT management (English, Dutch)
IT Service Management Best Practices, volumes 1, 2, 3 and 4 (Dutch)
ITSM from hell! (English)
ITSM from hell based on Not ITIL (English)
ITSMP - The IT Strategy Management Process (English)
Metrics for IT Service Management (English)
Service Management Process Maps (English)
Six Sigma for IT Management (English)
Six Sigma for IT Management – A Pocket Guide (English)

MOF/MSF
MOF - Microsoft Operations Framework, A Pocket Guide (Dutch, English, French, German, Japanese)
MSF - Microsoft Solutions Framework, A Pocket Guide (English, German)

For the latest information on VHP publications, visit our website: www.vanharen.net

The EFQM Excellence Model
For Assessing Organizational Performance

A Management Guide

Chris Hakes

Colofon

Title:	The EFQM Excellence Model
	For Assessing Organizational Performance – A Management Guide
Author:	Chris Hakes (Leadership Agenda Ltd)
Editor:	Jayne Wilkinson
Publisher:	Van Haren Publishing, Zaltbommel, www.vanharen.net
ISBN(13):	978 90 8753 027 3
Print:	First edition, first impression, June 2007
Layout and design:	CO2 Premedia bv, Amersfoort - NL
Copyright:	2007, Van Haren Publishing / Leadership Agenda Ltd

All content in this document is based on the EFQM Excellence Model. This Model is a core component of EFQM added value for the European business community. This book reproduces the so called *'upper level'* of the Model including the Model diagrams, the names of the criteria and criterion parts in their original form. For consistency with the full EFQM Model these elements of the Model are totally unchanged and EFQM copyright to these parts of this publication is hereby fully acknowledged: *'Copyright © 1999 – 2007 EFQM'*. Many additional and informative model-related publications can be obtained from EFQM via www.efqm.org

All other texts describing how to apply the Model and examples of good practices, that will enable readers to learn from what leaders in excellent organizations have done, are the work and views of the Author with copyright being assigned to the publisher. *'Copyright © 2007 Chris Hakes, Leadership Agenda Limited, UK.'* Additional leadership development materials of the Author can be obtained from www.leadershipagenda.com

The approach taken in this book is deliberately practical, it is informed by hands-on experience working with and analyzing the success of several EFQM Excellence Award winners, and a very broad range of organizations in the Public Sector. We hope we have succeeded in writing the book in a language of 'business' which we hope and believe will be relevant to all organizations, public or private, large or small. Clearly not *all* practices described will be relevant for *all* organizations and we rely on readers applying commonsense to contextualise the practices and their relevance for their own organization.

For any further enquiries about Van Haren Publishing, please send an e-mail to: info@vanharen.net

Although this publication has been composed with most care, author nor editor can accept any liability for damage caused by possible errors and/or incompleteness in this publication.

No part of this publication may be reproduced in any form by print, photo print, microfilm or any other means without written permission by the publisher.

Introduction and Acknowledgements

For a long time I was determined *not* to write this book. For many years, in the period 1993 to 1999, I authored publications on the then-entitled technique of 'Self Assessment', first published by Chapman and Hall, and then by Blackwell's and others, all now out of print and dated, in my mind, by their titles alone. Those books contained overviews of the history and evolution of what were then called Business Excellence Models, detailed analyzes of the various ways by which organizations could 'self-assess' their performance against such models, and a *simple* tool kit to enable them to do assessments against the EFQM (then known as the European Foundation for Quality Management) Excellence Model.

I had thought that the days of using such simple techniques were gone, but how wrong I was. Many organizations appear to have evolved from *simple* but effective techniques of performance assessment to rigorous but overly complex methodologies (and are now seeking a path back). Additionally, awareness of the benefits of such assessments is leading new generations of users to seek practical ways to do it. Anyway, the fact is that, after frequent requests to reprint the pro-forma approaches contained in the original handbooks, I've given in. This publication is the result.

This practical management guide gives only a simple review of the history and evolution of the EFQM Excellence Model and of the related approaches that it contains (as much freely available details can be obtained from sources such as www.efqm.org and many other openly available internet sources), but first time readers may appreciate noting that:

- EFQM is a not-for-profit membership foundation. Founded in 1989 by the CEOs of prominent European businesses. EFQM is a hub of globally-minded organizations in all sizes, sectors, both private and public, seeking to learn from each other and to improve their performance.
- EFQM is the creator of the prestigious EFQM Excellence Award which recognizes the very top performing European organizations each year.
- Perhaps most importantly, EFQM is the guardian of the 'EFQM Excellence Model' which provides organizations with a framework within which they can achieve and measure their success. The pro-forma assessment techniques in this book are based on techniques founded on this model.

I make no academic or research-based claims for this work, nor do I suggest exclusivity of thinking for the ideas tabled here; all I can assure you is that there are many users and several winners of the EFQM Excellence Award who have benefited from learning the proven good practices listed in the pro-formas and finding simple ways to assess themselves and their progress against them.

Finally, I would like to acknowledge and thank all those who have assisted, persisted, influenced, or generally helped to maintain my sanity during the production of this book. Particular thanks are due to friends and colleagues at EFQM and other global or regional awards administrations, along with my clients, with whom the learning journey has always been a two-way experience and, for me at least, a great pleasure. It is an old saying that, 'there is no finish-line in the race to excellence – the race never ends'. Sometimes, however, it is important for some to remember to begin the race and for others to renew the vigour with which they compete. I hope this book can help you begin or renew your journey to excellence.

May 2007, Chris Hakes

Content

Introduction and Acknowledgements V
Content VII
Why should you consider using the EFQM Excellence Model? 1
The Development of EFQM and its Excellence Model 2
EFQM and its Networks today 7
The Concepts behind the EFQM Excellence Model 11
EFQM Excellence Model content and structure 15
A five step plan for an effective Assessment of your organizations performance against
the EFQM Excellence Model 22
    Step 1. Build understanding of and commitment to the Model 22
    Step 2. Be clear, from the start, on your reasons for doing it 23
    Step 3. Be clear on the part of the organization you are going to assess and
             its strategic context 24
    Step 4. Choose and use an effective method of Assessment 26
    Step 5: Conclude Actions Arising 28
Appendix 1: A set of x32 Analysis Pro-Forma's 30
Appendix 2: Scoring Tools 96
Appendix 3: Comparison Tables showing 104 Applicants in period 2004-2006 104

Why should you consider using the EFQM Excellence Model?

Why should you consider using the EFQM Excellence Model?

The world's capital markets are becoming increasingly focused on the anticipated future or potential earnings of commercial organizations, as well as the value of their current, tangible assets and past successes. For all organizations, the processes by which success is evaluated are changing. For public sector organizations, governments, acting as the majority shareholders, are typically imposing ever-increasing challenges for enhanced efficiency, accountability, and performance. An ability to respond in line with rapidly changing government policy is more important than ever before. To address such challenges, in a world filled with rapid complex change, turbulence and ambiguity, successful organizations are shifting from a position where they exploit their historical successes, resources and positions, to one where their ability to sense a new opportunity/risk, and to respond to it in a timely and effectively way, is key.

> "We have learned that ... the past will be a poor guide to the future and that we shall forever be dealing with unanticipated events. Given that scenario, organizations will need individuals who delight in the unknown."
>
> Charles Handy

Increasingly organizations and leaders of the future will be able to make sense, meaning and opportunity out of the flood of signals received from the broader environment, will bring their creativity to bear in developing innovative opportunities, products and services from this analysis, and will align their people, organizations and processes with such new opportunities with effectiveness and appropriate speed.

> "In the old economy, the challenge for management was to make product. Now the challenge for management is to make sense."
>
> John Seely Brown

Effectively addressing such challenges, in today's world, has significant consequences for both individuals and organizations. Harmonising the behaviours and expectations of people within the systems and environment in which we expect them to operate is key, for it is the behaviours of individuals, their collective relationships and the processes they work within, that creates clarity, unity of purpose and the environment, in which an organization and its people perform, excel or fail.

"The most neglected leadership role is the designer of the ship."
Peter Senge

Maintaining world class levels of performance for the 'ship' above (of the processes to be *aligned* within the organization, the data streams for *sensing opportunity/risk* and the people and 'culture' of the organization necessary to ensure effective *response*) requires innovation and ever evolving ways of thinking and leading. It means constantly reviewing, even totally challenging, the status quo.

> "Some men see things as they are and say why. I dream things that never were and say why not."
>
> Robert Kennedy

To be successful in today's world many leading organizations adopt management frameworks and policy deployment mechanisms within which the values, attitudes, beliefs and behaviours of individuals can be understood, be in harmony and develop, in alignment with the goals, visions and aspirations of the organization. It is in this context that many organizations believe Excellence models have a role and, if in Europe they look towards Brussels and the EFQM Excellence Model for support.

The Development of EFQM and its Excellence Model

1950: In the early 1950s, the Union of Japanese Scientists and Engineers (JUSE) instituted the 'Deming Prize' to recognize both organizations and individuals who had made an exemplary contribution to the performance and excellence of their organizations. While the Deming Prize was undoubtedly the first recognizable 'Excellence Model', its adoption as an internal self-assessment process, within global organizations, was generally low outside Japan. For today's status and further insights visit http://www.juse.or.jp/e/deming/04.html

1983: In the US, a White House Conference on Productivity was held, with keynote speeches from President Reagan, Vice President Bush (Snr) and Commerce Secretary Malcolm Baldrige. The report published following the conference opened with a very blunt headline statement: *"America is the most productive nation in the world, but its growth in productivity has faltered. Some of the factors contributing to slower productivity growth are within our control and some are not, but it is important that we respond to this challenge."* A long and wide-ranging debate ensued, and resulted in agreement from both political and business leaders that corporate performance excellence should be recognized through the establishment of a highly prestigious national award presented annually by the President. Thus, the Malcolm Baldrige National Quality Award (MBNQA) was launched in 1988. The Award was first presented in 1988 to Motorola, Westinghouse and Globe Metallurgical. It is based on the use of a transparent, widely communicated, performance Excellence model and has continued to the present day. For more insights go to: http://www.quality.nist.gov/

1988: The Presidents of 14 European companies came together to create the European Foundation for Quality Management. EFQM was formally established on 15 September 1988 in Brussels at the Chateau of Val Duchesse, where, thirty years earlier, the European Economic Community had begun. The Presidents of Bosch, BT, Bull, Ciba-Geigy, Dassault, Electrolux, Fiat, KLM, Nestlé, Olivetti, Philips, Renault, Sulzer and Volkswagen attended this important meeting and became the founders of EFQM.

1989: On 19 October 1989 in Montreux, EFQMs Mission, Vision and Objectives were officially presented. A policy document was signed by the Presidents of the 14 founding companies and the 53 co-founder companies. The EFQM mission was three-fold: to support the management of European companies as well as to stimulate and, where necessary, to assist all segments of the European community. EFQM planned to achieve these aims through becoming a not-for-profit network of member organizations and creating a prestigious business award to promote the use of a performance assessment framework.

1991: The EFQM Excellence Model was born. From 1988 to 1991, the newly established EFQM focused its activities on and around the development of a member network and the EFQM Excellence Model. It was intended that the model be used as the framework against which applicants for a European Excellence Award could be judged. The work brought together a small core team of 10 so-called 'thinkers' supported by approximately 300 in-company experts from across Europe consisting primarily of the founders and early key corporate members of EFQM.

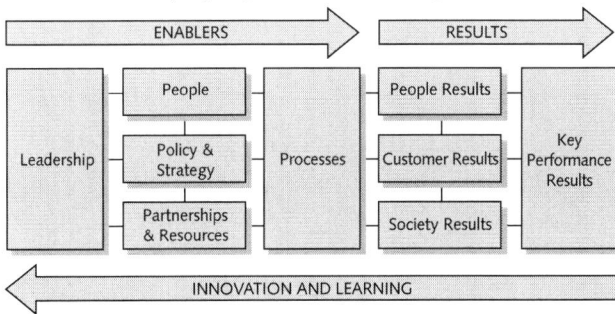

Figure 1: The EFQM Excellence Model (copyright: EFQM)

The criteria for the EFQM Excellence Model were developed by taking the best from other business standards and models, including the Deming Prize, the MBNQA process and through lengthy consultation with leaders in the business community. The criteria established by this approach thus reflected a consensus of what best practice looked like at the time (and this has been maintained by periodic reviews ever since). Although the ongoing annual award presentations are perhaps the most visible outcome of this work, in practice, the vast majority of users of the Model do so within their organizations, with no intent to apply for an award. Part of the ongoing success and popularity of the Model is due to the development of case studies of excellence, based on real-life examples. In addition, assessor training is widely available, and serves to develop and calibrate teams of assessors, who can apply this learning both to their own organizations and to award applicants.

1992: The first European Quality Award was presented to Rank Xerox, by the King of Spain at the EFQM Forum in Madrid.

1995: In the beginning, EFQM tended to focus on commercial organizations which were large businesses and their subsidiaries. But after the first year of the award, it became apparent that the Model was equally applicable to the Public Sector and to Small and Medium Enterprises (SMEs). EFQM, supported by the European Commission began to encourage such organizations to use the EFQM Excellence Model and potentially to apply for the European Excellence Award.

EFQM and its Networks today

EFQM and its Networks today

Partner Networks:

Since 1991, agreements have been signed with national not-for-profit Excellence Organizations which now form the network of EFQM National Partner Organizations (NPOs). They have similar aims and objectives to EFQM and there are currently 24 NPOs. These NPOs represent EFQM within their countries and provide a range of services to their members and customers in the local language.

National Partner Organization contacts:

AUSTRIA: http://www.oevq.at and http://www.afqm.at
BELGIUM: http://www.bbest.be and http://www.vck.be
CZECH REPUBLIC: e-mail: hnatek@centrum.cz
DENMARK: http://www.cfl.dk
FINLAND: http://www.laatukeskus.fi
FRANCE: e-mail: philippe.bianchi@afnor.fr
GERMANY: http://www.dgq.de
GREECE: http://www.eede.gr
HUNGARY: e-mail: info@mik.hu
IRELAND: http://www.eiqa.com
ITALY: http://www.aicq.it
POLAND: e-mail: pcbc@pcbc.gov.pl or ara@kig.pl or tadeusz.buchacz@umbrella.org.pl
PORTUGAL: http://www.apq.pt
RUSSIA: http://www.cepvok.ru or http://www.mirq.ru
SLOVENIA: http://www.mirs.si

SPAIN: http://www.clubexcelencia.org
SWEDEN: http://www.siq.se
SWITZERLAND: http://www.saq.ch or http://www.arq.ch
TURKEY: http://www.kalder.org
UKRAINE: http://www.qualitykiev.org
UNITED KINGDOM: http://www.quality-foundation.co.uk
NORTHERN IRELAND: http://www.cforc.org
SCOTLAND: http://www.qualityscotland.co.uk
WALES: http://www.walesqualitycentre.org.uk.
Full details of NPO contact points are listed at http://www.efqm.org.

Knowledge Networking:

One advantage of using the EFQM Excellence Model is that it provides a framework and common language by which to learn and seek performance insights from outside of your organization. The EFQM Knowledge network provides contact with over one thousand organizations which operate globally across various sectors. EFQM maintains a strong knowledge base in the area of performance excellence and continuous improvement, most of it formatted around the 'language' of the EFQM Excellence Model. A comprehensive website with links to all of this knowledge can be found at www.efqm.org.

A sub-site called 'Excellence One' is their key knowledge sharing area. Here they package a compilation of recent articles on management topics, best practices from various industries, over 400 articles on the implementation of business excellence and a number of learning tools and resources. Any user is able to see the basic level of information available; if you register your contact details, you will be able to read the most recently published articles; if your Organization is an EFQM Member, you have access to all the tools and resources.

This database includes:
- benchmarking Reports and Benchmarking Data
- a Good Practice Database
- over 400 articles on excellent management practices
- process Survey Tools
- extracts from Award Winners 'Applications' and assessments
- video interviews from CEOs
- presentations on EFQM for your own use

You can access this source at http://excellenceone.efqm.org

Key Facts:

- EFQM continues to operate an annual European Excellence Award; 2006 winners are BMW Group Chassis and Driveline Systems Production, Grundfos A/S, TNT Express GmbH, St. Mary's College Londonderry.
- A 'Levels of Excellence' scheme engages organizations at the early stages of their journey to excellence (for more details see http//www.efqm.org).
- The EFQM member network is composed of approximately 1,000 organizations in 35 countries.
- Research shows that 60% of Europe's largest companies use the EFQM Excellence Model to improve their business performance.

The Concepts behind the EFQM Excellence Model

The Concepts behind the EFQM Excellence Model

Underpinning the EFQM Excellence Model, on which this Management Guide is based, is a set of eight 'core values'. These so-called 'Fundamental Concepts' created by EFQM in the early 1990s, were then, and continue to be, informed-renewed by their networks and users. They thereby represent a consensus on the key management principles and beliefs that will drive the sustainable success of European organizations. The Excellence Model itself (see the next chapter) is simply a framework to translate these concepts into action. For an organization to maximize the benefits of adopting the EFQM Excellence Model, a management team must first ensure that it is comfortable with these concepts. Clearly, if these concepts are not fully understood and accepted then progress with adopting the Model will be difficult and potentially meaningless.

The Fundamental Concepts are:

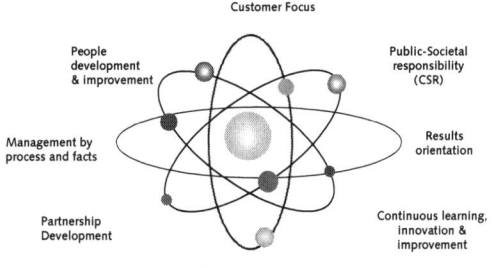

A detailed and free brochure, further describing these Fundamental Concepts can be downloaded from www.efqm.org.

Figure 2: Fundamental Concepts of Excellence

The eight Fundamental Concepts of excellence that underpin the EFQM Excellence Model can be summarised as follows:

1. **Leadership and Constancy of Purpose:** Excellence is about visionary and inspirational leadership, coupled with constancy of purpose.

> *"If you don't know where you are going" the Scarecrow said to Dorothy, "it doesn't matter which road you take."*
> *The Wonderful Wizard of Oz, L. Frank Baum*

2. **Continuous Learning, Innovation and Improvement:** Excellence is about challenging the status quo and effecting change by utilising learning to create innovation and improvement opportunities.

> *"We'll have to learn from the mistakes that others make. We can't live long enough to make them all ourselves."*
> *Anon*

3. **People Development and Involvement:** Excellence is about maximizing the contribution of employees through their development and involvement.

> *"The task of the leader is to get his people from where they are to where they have not been"*
> *Henry Kissinger*

4. **Partnership Development:** Excellence is about developing and maintaining value-adding partnerships.

5. **Customer Focus:** Excellence is about creating sustainable customer value.

6. **Management by Processes and Facts:** Excellence is about managing the organization through a set of interdependent and interrelated systems, processes and facts.

> "Most of what we call management consists of making it difficult for people to get their jobs done"
>
> Peter Drucker

7. **Corporate Social Responsibility:** Excellence is about exceeding the minimum regulatory framework in which the organization operates, and to strive to understand and respond to the expectations of their stakeholders in society.
8. **Results Orientation:** Excellence is about achieving results that delight all the organization's stakeholders.

> "The first responsibility of a leader is to define reality"
>
> Max DePree **The Art of Leadership**

EFQM Excellence Model content and structure

EFQM Excellence Model content and structure

The EFQM Excellence Model translates these eight Fundamental Concepts of management into a dynamic and non prescriptive operational model, by which performance can be assessed.

At the highest level the model consists of nine criteria (see Figure 1):
- **five key enablers of excellence (leadership, policy and strategy, people management, resources and processes).**
  These criteria provide ways to assess what is being done in the organization which, if effective, should be dynamically driving excellence in
- **the four results criteria (for customers, people, society and the business stakeholders)**
  These criteria provide ways to assess what has been achieved.

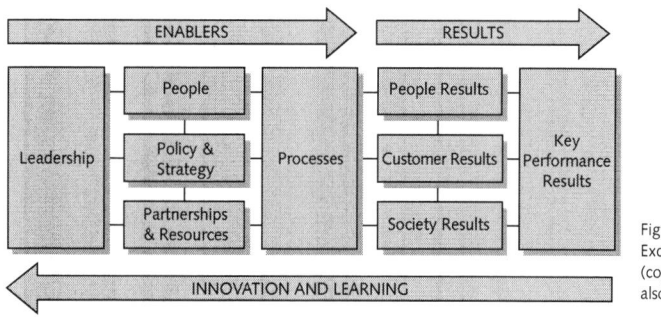

Figure 1: The EFQM Excellence Model (copyright: EFQM). See also page 5.

The arrows in Figure 1 emphasize the dynamic nature of the Model. The Model and its related scoring process (see Appendix 2) is a dynamic system. Innovation and learning must be present continually, to refine and improve the enablers that will, in turn, be likely to lead to improved future results.

Each of the nine criteria has a definition, which explains the high level meaning of that criterion. Beneath the nine criteria is a framework of 32 criterion parts; the criterion parts collectively provide a more detailed description of the Model.

The 32 analysis pro-formas in Appendix 1 provide the detailed description of each of the 32 criterion parts, they indicate how they relate to each other and list examples of good practices that leading organizations use to address the issues raised.

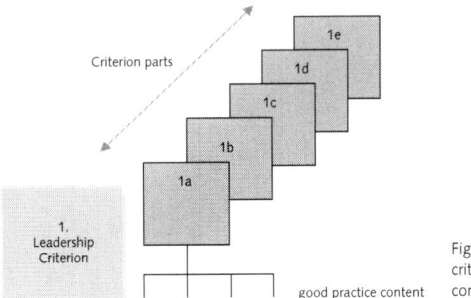

Figure 3: Relationships between criterion parts and good practice content

So, for example for criterion 1, readers wishing to understand the full meaning of the criterion parts for leadership should first read Appendix 1, where the criterion parts 1a through to 1e are fully described, further flow diagrams provided and good practice insights given.

At the highest level nine criteria are defined as follows:

Note the light grey shaded boxes show the within criterion linkages, the dark grey shaded boxes show key related criteria that should be borne in mind during assessments.

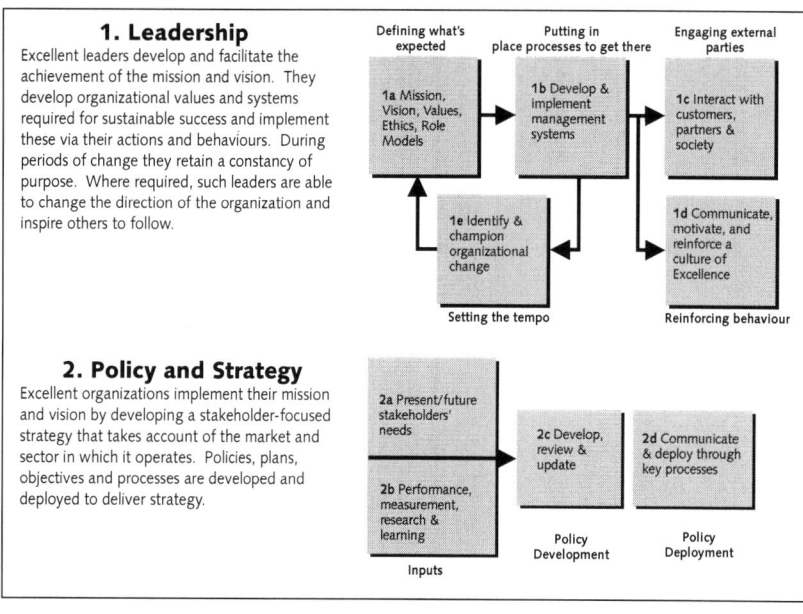

1. Leadership

Excellent leaders develop and facilitate the achievement of the mission and vision. They develop organizational values and systems required for sustainable success and implement these via their actions and behaviours. During periods of change they retain a constancy of purpose. Where required, such leaders are able to change the direction of the organization and inspire others to follow.

2. Policy and Strategy

Excellent organizations implement their mission and vision by developing a stakeholder-focused strategy that takes account of the market and sector in which it operates. Policies, plans, objectives and processes are developed and deployed to deliver strategy.

3. People

Excellent organizations manage, develop and release the full potential of their people at an individual, team-based and organizational level. They promote fairness and equality, and involve and empower their people. They care for, communicate, reward and recognize, in a way that motivates staff and builds commitment to using their skills and knowledge for the benefit of the organization.

4. Partnerships and Resources

Excellent organizations plan to manage external partnerships, suppliers and internal resources in order to support policy and strategy and the effective operation of processes. During planning, and whilst managing partnerships and resources, they balance the current and future needs of the organization, the community, and the environment.

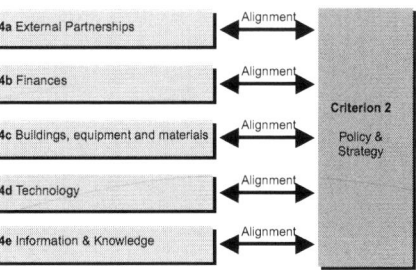

5. Processes

Excellent organizations design, manage and improve processes in order to fully satisfy, and generate increasing value for, customers and other stakeholders.

6. Customer Results

Excellent organizations comprehensively measure and achieve outstanding results with respect to their customers

7. People Results

Excellent organizations comprehensively measure and achieve outstanding results with respect to their people..

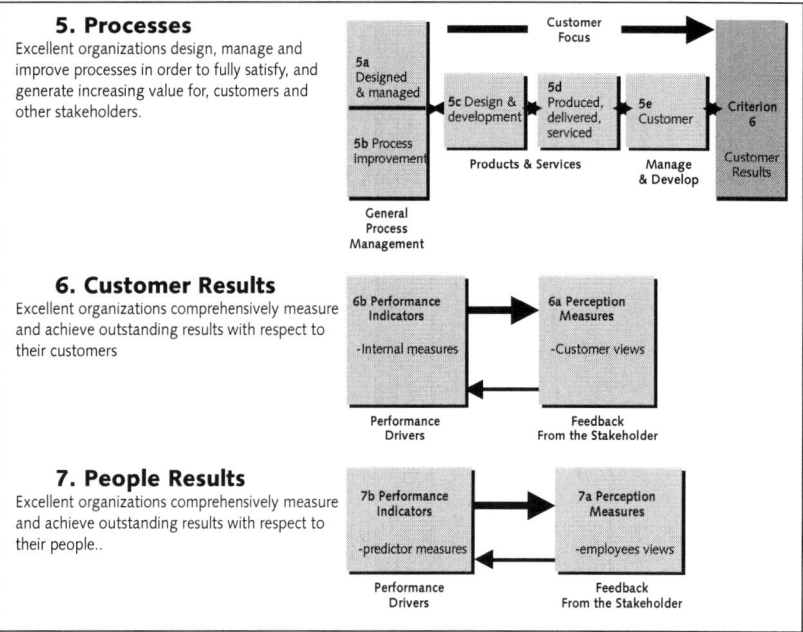

8. Society Results
Excellent organizations comprehensively measure and achieve outstanding results with respect to society.

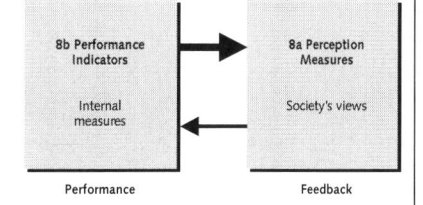

8b Performance Indicators	→	8a Perception Measures
Internal measures	←	Society's views

Performance   Feedback

9. Key Performance Results
Excellent organizations comprehensively measure and achieve outstanding results with respect to the key elements of their policy and strategy.

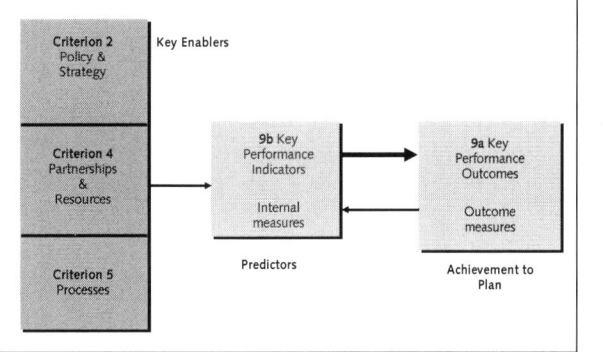

Criterion 2 Policy & Strategy — Key Enablers

Criterion 4 Partnerships & Resources

Criterion 5 Processes

9b Key Performance Indicators	→	9a Key Performance Outcomes
Internal measures	←	Outcome measures

Predictors   Achievement to Plan

A five step plan for an effective Assessment of your organization's performance against the EFQM Excellence Model

Step 1. Build understanding of and commitment to the Model

The EFQM Excellence Model provides a holistic approach to managing for improvement, and so is most successful when it has the full support of everyone in the Executive team of an organization.

To achieve this, over time, a systematic plan to raising awareness and dealing with any perceived barriers will be key. Such plans could include:

- providing reading materials, such as those published by EFQM and or translations made by National or Regional Award schemes using the EFQM Excellence Model;
- circulating copies of a published award-winning submissions;
- preparing a presentation on how the Model might relate to the organization;
- attending training courses;
- visits or conferences to meet face-to face with executives and/or organizations who have been using the Model for some time; and/or
- carrying out a simple first assessment; many users of the Model, when looking back at their early experiences comment that full awareness/understanding of both the process and its benefits was not fully attained until they undertook their first assessment.

Again, further supportive resources are available at www.efqm.org

Step 2. Be clear, from the start, on your reasons for doing it

After a period of learning-awareness leading to some degree of understanding and commitment there comes a time to undertake your first assessment. Although your answer to the question 'why are we doing this?' may change over time (as you become more experienced and robust with your assessments), it is vital to be clear on this at the start, particularly for your first assessment.

Organizations enjoy many potential benefits as a result of undertaking assessments using the EFQM Excellence Model. These include providing:

- a proven, structured, fact-based technique to identifying and **Assessing your Organization's Strengths and Areas for Improvement** and measuring its progress periodically;
- a way to **Compare Performance** with others;
- a method that helps identify **Good Practices,** both internally and externally;
- as the basis for creating a **Common Vocabulary,** way of thinking and method to **Educate People** in your organization on the Fundamental Concepts of Excellence and how they relate to their responsibilities;
- a way to draw from and **Co-ordinate the Contributions of all Stakeholders** in a way that enhances a mutual learning and trust culture; and
- as a structure to help **Integrate the various projects and Improvement Initiatives** into your normal operational systems.

> *"Being able to learn faster than the competition may be the only sustainable advantage"*
> *Arie de Geus. ('The Living Company')*

EFQM uses the term 'Self-Assessment' to describe a self (organizationally) led application of the Model. The EFQM definition of Self-Assessment is as follows: *'Self-Assessment is a comprehensive, systematic and regular review by an organization of its activities and results referenced against the EFQM Excellence Model. The Self-Assessment process allows the organization to discern clearly its strengths and areas in which improvements can be made and culminates in planned improvement actions that are then monitored for progress.'*

Perhaps the last sentence is key and if you are not able to drive the result of the assessment activity to 'actions' perhaps you need to reconsider your thinking.

Step 3. Be clear the part of the organization you are going to assess and its strategic context

Right at the start of the project, it is essential to scope the assessment by defining the boundaries of the organization to be assessed and being clear on the strategic context for the assessment.

It may be, for example, that the organization is a division or sub-unit within a larger enterprise, with full accountability for some of its activities, but taking some of its internal services from the parent company; in this case the answers to some of the following 'Key Factors' may be complex.

To help you to ensure that these boundaries are clear in your mind (and we suggest also for you to obtain agreement from all those involved at the start), we suggest you create a *short document* (2-3 pages maximum) to list response to what EFQM calls 'Key Factors' that should be used to give strategic context to the application of the model.

There are five Key Factors to consider. Key Factors are those key facts about your organization which help to give appropriate strategic context to the way in which you apply the model in Assessment. See Figure 3.

KF1: Organizational definition/environment

Create a short list of the key facts that define your organization: history, values, vision and mission, its geographical sites, people, etc.

KF2: What is your performance improvement system?
List your key approaches to improving the performance of your organization: what tools are used?

KF3: Organizational relationships
List those who you regard as current and potential stakeholders: key partners, key suppliers, relationship with parent organization (if appropriate), internal customer supplier relationships, etc.

KF4: Competitive environment
List current and potential markets/intermediaries/competitors/customers, your position in different markets, the key customer needs, segmentations, major customers, use of distributors, etc.

KF5: Your main strategic challenges?
List key risks and opportunities in current and future value propositions: which ones are already achieved, what are the ones ahead in the near and further future?

Strategic context for Assessments:

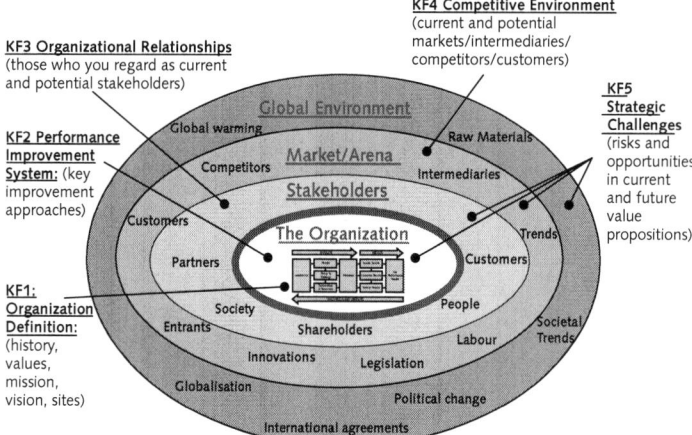

Figure 4: Strategic context for assessments

Step 4. Choose and use an effective method of Assessment

There is no definitive answer to the question 'Which is the right way to apply the EFQM Excellence Model to perform an Assessment of my organization?', the culture and structure of the organization, as well as the benefits desired should influence the decision as to which particular Assessment technique to adopt at any given moment in time. Options are often segmented into the following categories:

- **Use of Questionnaires** - This technique can be one of the least resource intensive and can be completed very quickly. It is an excellent method for gathering information on the perceptions of people within an organization. Some organizations use simple yes/no questionnaires; others adopt slightly more sophisticated versions that use a rating scale. Questionnaires can also be used as a method for widespread data gathering in support of a more detailed assessment technique. Examples can be downloaded at www.efqm.org
- **Assessment Workshops** - This is typically a facilitated event of between one and one-and-a-half days, that involves members of a team in a discussion and decision-making process linked to assessing evidence on data presented against each part of the model and reaching consensus on strengths and areas for improvement. Subsequently, a second discussion and decision-making process is used to prioritise the list of potential improvement actions, assign ownership and agree timescales for delivery of the improvements.
- **Award Simulation** - This technique is effectively a replication of entering for the EFQM Excellence Award. It involves writing for the individual unit or whole organization undertaking the Assessment a submission document presenting your organization's achievements across a range of areas relating to each sub-criteria of the EFQM Excellence Model.

The use of assessment data gathering pro-formas can help inform all approaches –This management guide contains a series of 32 pro-formas, one for each criterion part. By following the self explanatory steps on the forms in Appendix 1 and using a scoring approach as described in Appendix 2 users of this management guide can help inform any chosen method of assessment.

We recommend that a good first assessment approach is to use the pro-formas in this book to prepare for and undertake an Assessment workshop. With this approach, the Executive team (or a group of key players) comes together in a workshop environment to undertake a 'live' assessment over a one to one-and-a-half day period.

During the workshop, the team compiles agreed lists of strengths and areas for improvement against each of the elements of the Model. With appropriate facilitation, the team members can be prompted to ensure that they have addressed and scored/analyzed all the relevant areas.

Step 5. Conclude Actions Arising

Once an assessment is completed, may have created a long list of strengths and areas for improvement. A good next step is to use a systematic approach to prioritisation and action planning.

If you have used the pro-forma's in Appendix 1 of this book the last question on each of the x32 pro-formas will have prompted you to assess strategic importance on a scale from 'not relevant' to 'useful' to 'important' to 'critical'. You will also have a % score for each criterion part. The next step is to plot each criterion part by its likely strategic impact, and the criterion part score you obtained, on a two-axis matrix. The horizontal axis should run from 0%, on the left, to the highest criterion part score you achieved in the assessment on the right. This should be bisected by the vertical axis, representing strategic importance at the halfway point.

It is likely that the plot will populate all four segments. In the top right, there are the high impact, high scoring criterion parts. These criterion parts are your sources of strength, and should be reinforced. The 'vital few' areas for improvement are in the top left quadrant. These are of high impact on the business, but are scoring at a low level and should be the subject of further debate and action.

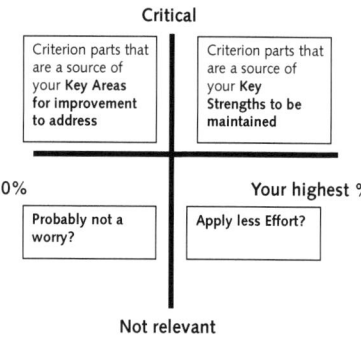

Figure 5: Criterion part score matrix

Final Conclusions:

After a first assessment, you will have to decide whether to integrate the approaches experienced into the existing management systems of the business or whether to run EFQM Model Assessments/ Excellence as a 'project' for a little while. In practice, this is often an evolutionary process. Many organizations start with an 'Excellence project' in order to satisfy themselves of its value, and to learn more, before integrating it into the existing planning cycle. If you choose a project-based approach, it is a good practice to create a project steering team. The role of the project steering team could include:

- creating, and managing, the overall project plan;
- raising awareness of Excellence throughout the organization;
- training as assessors and participating in further assessments;
- facilitating and co-ordinating improvement projects and reporting on progress.

Appendix 1: A set of x32 Analysis Pro-Forma's

Undertaking a workshop assessment is an ideal way to gain commitment to using the EFQM Excellence Model, increase understanding of the technique and put a first 'stake in the ground' (a first estimate) as to how well the organization scores. A set of pro-forma tools can help you obtain/review your thinking in advance of a workshop analysis day. This following x32 set of pro-forma pages are a tried and tested format developed originally in the early 1990s, but now updated to include good practices distilled from EFQM Award winners over those years. A series of success factors (things you should do or have) to guide your planning of a workshop are below:

Pre-Workshop	During Workshop	Post-Workshop
– Clear roles/responsibilities – Sound preparation – Project management – Data gathering finished – Understanding of the Model – Commitment to do it – Understanding of process – Circulated composite lists and analyzes beforehand	– Keep to the facts – Planned agenda – Start with 'easier' criterion – Meeting discipline – Listen to others' opinions – Not about blame – Environment: (off-site) – Do not try to problem-solve at this stage – Equipment – Capturing of the output in a good form – Teamwork – Facilitation – Agree next steps before leaving	– Ownership of outcomes – Prioritization process agreed – Review process of Self-Assessment – Review progress on action plans

Figure 6: Success factors for workshop assessments

In the following pages each pro-forma leads you through a self explanatory series of steps to analyze your performance against each criterion part. At the beginning of each, there is a diagram to help you understand what to assess, followed by a number of good practice insights to help you learn what leaders in excellent organizations do for the criterion part you are analyzing. This is followed by a series of steps to help you analyze your own organizations performance.

For Enablers, complete steps 1 through to 9:
   Step 1: Understand what to Assess
   Step 2: Learn from what leaders in excellent organizations do for the criterion part
   Step 3-6: Analyze your own organizations key activity-behaviour for the criterion part
   Step 7: List your personal analysis of your strengths and areas for improvement
   Step 8: Score the analysis
   Step 9: Rank the strategic importance of the analysis

For Results, complete steps 1 to 11:
   Step 1: Understand what to Assess
   Step 2: Learn from what leaders in excellent organizations do for the criterion part
   Step 3-8: Analyze your own organizations measures and achievements for the criterion part
   Step 9: List your personal analysis of your strengths and areas for improvement
   Step 10: Score the analysis
   Step 11: Rank the strategic importance of the analysis

Guidance on a simple scoring approach is given in Appendix 2 Comparative data on the scored performance of EFQM Award applicants is given in Appendix 3.

After individually completing the pro-forma assessments in Appendix 1 remember to take your analysis through to steps 4 and 5 of the five step process described earlier. Analysis without conclusion and action is an easy trap to fall into, but a poor outcome of your efforts.

Leadership 1a

Step 1. Understand what to assess:

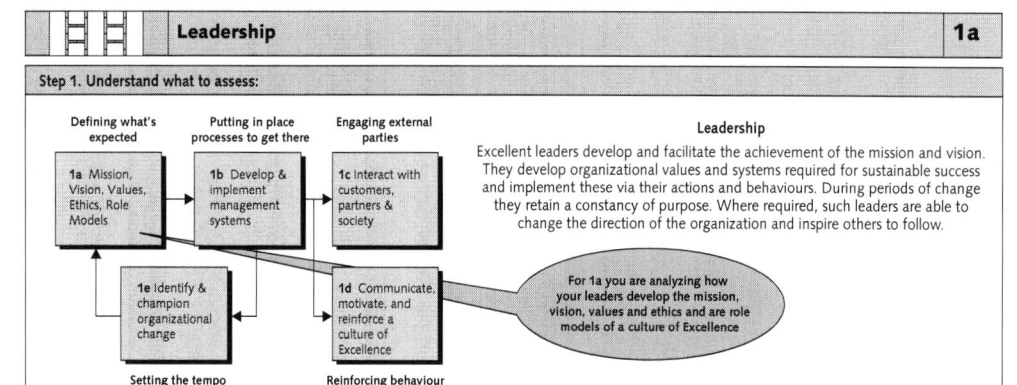

Defining what's expected
- 1a Mission, Vision, Values, Ethics, Role Models

Putting in place processes to get there
- 1b Develop & implement management systems

Engaging external parties
- 1c Interact with customers, partners & society

Setting the tempo
- 1e Identify & champion organizational change

Reinforcing behaviour
- 1d Communicate, motivate, and reinforce a culture of Excellence

Leadership
Excellent leaders develop and facilitate the achievement of the mission and vision. They develop organizational values and systems required for sustainable success and implement these via their actions and behaviours. During periods of change they retain a constancy of purpose. Where required, such leaders are able to change the direction of the organization and inspire others to follow.

For 1a you are analyzing how your leaders develop the mission, vision, values and ethics and are role models of a culture of Excellence

Step 2. Learn from what leaders in excellent organizations do for 1a:

They ensure that leaders at all levels of the organization:

i. Are collectively engaged in defining-reviewing **organizational missions, visions and values-ethics**

ii. Maximize the involvement of their people in the understanding, development, and **sharing of the organizations missions, visions and values-ethics**

iii. Target a **desired organizational climate**(s)

iv. Understand that there is **'no finish line in the race to excellence'** and visibly champion continual performances improvements (large and small, short term and long term) in this context

v. Have policies and plans to **endorse improvement activities**, through, for example, leaders acting as improvement team sponsors, or participants, or communicating successful improvements made

vi. **Personally use** the improvement methodologies provided for their people, and make this involvement visible (as a role model activity) whenever possible

vii. Are clear on what are **role model leadership behaviours** for the organization leaders

viii. Find ways to measure their **personal leadership effectiveness** and have development plans to improve it

APPENDIX 1: A SET OF X32 ANALYSIS PRO-FORMA'S

Steps 3-5: Analyze Key Activity-Behaviour for this Criterion-Part

3: Approaches	4: Deployment	5: Assessment and Review
List the processes and behaviours that impact on this criterion part.	*To what extent do you intend to deploy each? Has this been effectively achieved?*	*How and how often do you review the effectiveness of each activity and the overall mix of approaches?*

Step 6: List the key actions and improvements that arose from the review activities you listed in step 5

Step 7: Conclude an analysis of your key strengths and areas for improvement for this Criterion-Part

Strengths:	Areas for Improvement:

Step 8: Score your Analysis

| Approach: | % | Deployment: | % | Assessment & Review: | % | Overall: | % |

Step 9: Tick one of the options to rank the strategic importance of addressing the issues arising from the analysis above

| ☐ Not relevant | ☐ Useful | ☐ Important | ☐ Critical to our success |

Leadership 1b

Step 1. Understand what to assess:

Defining what's expected
- 1a Mission, Vision, Values, Ethics, Role Models

Putting in place processes to get there
- 1b Develop & implement management systems
- 1e Identify & champion organizational change

Setting the tempo

Engaging external parties
- 1c Interact with customers, partners & society
- 1d Communicate, motivate, and reinforce a culture of Excellence

Reinforcing behaviour

Leadership
Excellent leaders develop and facilitate the achievement of the mission and vision. They develop organizational values and systems required for sustainable success and implement these via their actions and behaviours. During periods of change they retain a constancy of purpose. Where required, such leaders are able to change the direction of the organization and inspire others to follow.

For 1b you are analyzing how your leaders are personally involved in ensuring the organizations management system is developed, implemented and continuously improved

Step 2. Learn from what leaders in excellent organizations do for 1b:

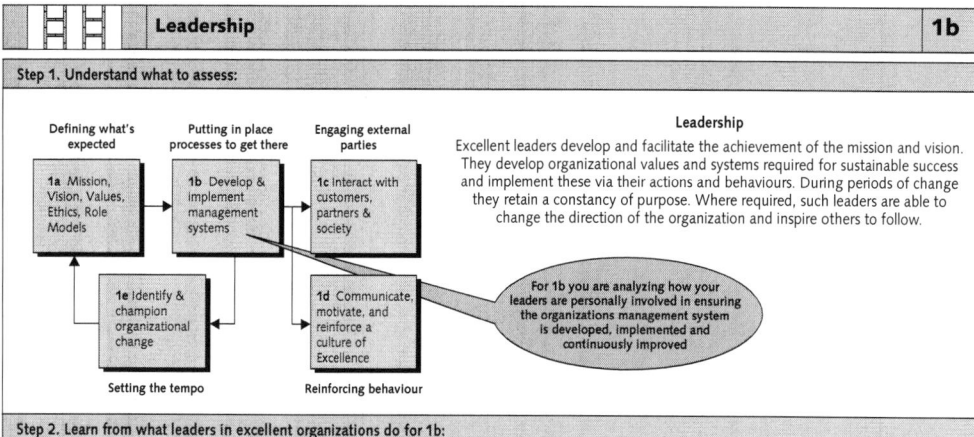

They ensure that leaders at all levels of the organization are engaged in:

i. Systematically defining-reviewing the organization's **governance, people and process structure** and its ability to support the delivery of the organizations current and foreseen aims
ii. Ensuring that defined **process structure of the organization has clear roles (ownership) assigned** to accountable people
iii. Making clear that all leaders have **formally appraised objectives** and targets related to the process and governance infrastructure of the business
iv. Ensuring that they define-maintain an effective performance management systems that is able to systematically review performance, monitor variance to plans and establish **timely and formal improvement activities if a performance is below standard (see also 2d, 3c)**
v. Understanding the **effectiveness of the mix of the approaches** above and make improvements with strategic agility (timeliness, response-reaction times) and innovation in mind

APPENDIX 1: A SET OF X32 ANALYSIS PRO-FORMA'S

Steps 3-5: Analyze Key Activity-Behaviour for this Criterion-Part		
3: Approaches	4: Deployment	5: Assessment and Review
List the processes and behaviours that impact on this criterion part.	*To what extent do you intend to deploy each? Has this been effectively achieved?*	*How and how often do you review the effectiveness of each activity and the overall mix of approaches?*

Step 6: List the key actions and improvements that arose from the review activities you listed in step 5

Step 7: Conclude an analysis of your key strengths and areas for improvement for this Criterion-Part	
Strengths:	Areas for Improvement:

Step 8: Score your Analysis			
Approach: %	Deployment: %	Assessment & Review: %	Overall: %
Step 9: Tick one of the options to rank the strategic importance of addressing the issues arising from the analysis above			
☐ Not relevant	☐ Useful	☐ Important	☐ Critical to our success

Leadership 1c

Step 1. Understand what to assess:

Defining what's expected
- 1a Mission, Vision, Values, Ethics, Role Models

Putting in place processes to get there
- 1b Develop & implement management systems

Engaging external parties
- 1c Interact with customers, partners & society

- 1e Identify & champion organizational change (Setting the tempo)
- 1d Communicate, motivate, and reinforce a culture of Excellence (Reinforcing behaviour)

Leadership
Excellent leaders develop and facilitate the achievement of the mission and vision. They develop organizational values and systems required for sustainable success and implement these via their actions and behaviours. During periods of change they retain a constancy of purpose. Where required, such leaders are able to change the direction of the organization and inspire others to follow.

For 1c you are analyzing how your leaders interact with customers, partners and representatives of society

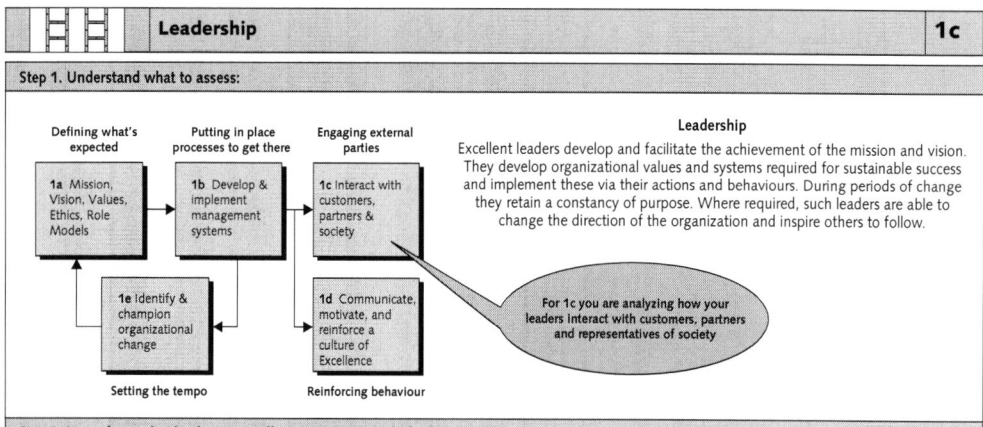

Step 2. Learn from what leaders in excellent organizations do for 1c:

They ensure that leaders at all levels of the organization are:

i. Assigned a formal, targeted responsibility to **focus on developing relationships with key stakeholders** (such as customers, key suppliers, partners, representatives of the wider community, and those with a corporate interest)
ii. **Meeting regularly** with these stakeholders and listen and respond to their needs;
iii. Co-ordinating a **systematic program of external learning visits**, so that leaders can obtain insights from external good practice (Conferences, Professional bodies, Universities, etc.)
iv. Presenting at seminars and conferences, and participate in visit schemes to **show their achievements/strategies/needs to others**
v. Promoting and sharing the organizations societal and **ethical values/behaviours**
vi. **Anticipating-addressing public concerns with current/future products and services** in a proactive manner
vii. Making effective communications **on issues observed and lessons learnt from all** external interactions
viii. Promoting the development of improvement teams to **tackle key issues** across internal and external organizational boundaries and recognising/promoting the successes of such teams

APPENDIX 1: A SET OF X32 ANALYSIS PRO-FORMA'S

Steps 3-5: Analyze Key Activity-Behaviour for this Criterion-Part		
3: Approaches	4: Deployment	5: Assessment and Review
List the processes and behaviours that impact on this criterion part.	*To what extent do you intend to deploy each? Has this been effectively achieved?*	*How and how often do you review the effectiveness of each activity and the overall mix of approaches?*

Step 6: List the key actions and improvements that arose from the review activities you listed in step 5

Step 7: Conclude an analysis of your key strengths and areas for improvement for this Criterion-Part

Strengths:	Areas for Improvement:

Step 8: Score your Analysis

Approach: %	Deployment: %	Assessment & Review: %	Overall: %

Step 9: Tick one of the options to rank the strategic importance of addressing the issues arising from the analysis above

☐ Not relevant	☐ Useful	☐ Important	☐ Critical to our success

Leadership 1d

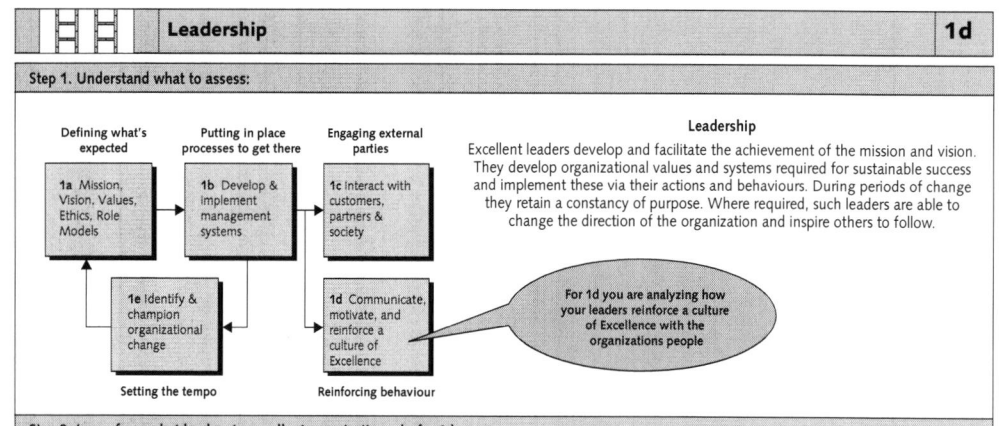

Step 1. Understand what to assess:

Defining what's expected
- 1a Mission, Vision, Values, Ethics, Role Models

Putting in place processes to get there
- 1b Develop & implement management systems

Engaging external parties
- 1c Interact with customers, partners & society

- 1e Identify & champion organizational change (Setting the tempo)
- 1d Communicate, motivate, and reinforce a culture of Excellence (Reinforcing behaviour)

Leadership
Excellent leaders develop and facilitate the achievement of the mission and vision. They develop organizational values and systems required for sustainable success and implement these via their actions and behaviours. During periods of change they retain a constancy of purpose. Where required, such leaders are able to change the direction of the organization and inspire others to follow.

For 1d you are analyzing how your leaders reinforce a culture of Excellence with the organizations people

Step 2. Learn from what leaders in excellent organizations do for 1d:

They ensure that leaders at all levels of the organization are deploying strategies, objectives and plans in a way which engages and motivates; this can include:

i. Reviewing team and individual performance to agreed targets-plans
ii. Giving **regular feedback** to their teams on overall business performance, and discussing its impact
iii. Ensuring that their people are **aware of competitor performance** and its potential impact;
iv. Supplementing formal mechanisms with regular **informal walkabouts** and discussions
v. Recording and formally **reviewing the messages, ideas and feedback** they receive from all of these activities, and ensuring that any actions they take are communicated back to the original source;
vi. Personally **acting within the frameworks of the organizations values-ethics** at all times, and making it clear that adoption of these values-ethics is a pre-requisite for advancement of any employee
vii. Creating a **spirit of trust**, experimentation and achievement by promoting success, constructively and openly acknowledging failure, and personally coaching improvement in those who are not fully achieving.
viii. Taking personal initiative to **recognize achievement and improvement** in ways which are meaningful to the organization, team and the individual (see also 3e)

APPENDIX 1: A SET OF X32 ANALYSIS PRO-FORMA'S

Steps 3-5: Analyze Key Activity-Behaviour for this Criterion-Part

3: Approaches	4: Deployment	5: Assessment and Review
List the processes and behaviours that impact on this criterion part.	*To what extent do you intend to deploy each? Has this been effectively achieved?*	*How and how often do you review the effectiveness of each activity and the overall mix of approaches?*

Step 6: List the key actions and improvements that arose from the review activities you listed in step 5

Step 7: Conclude an analysis of your key strengths and areas for improvement for this Criterion-Part

Strengths:	Areas for Improvement:

Step 8: Score your Analysis

Approach: %	Deployment: %	Assessment & Review: %	Overall: %

Step 9: Tick one of the options to rank the strategic importance of addressing the issues arising from the analysis above

☐ Not relevant	☐ Useful	☐ Important	☐ Critical to our success

Leadership — 1e

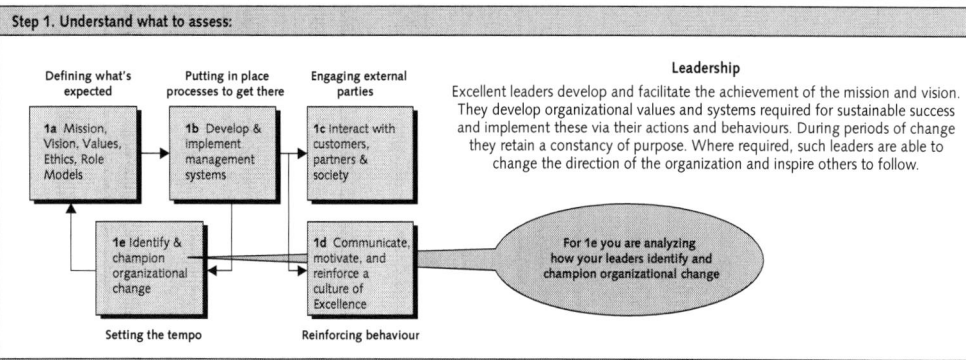

Step 1. Understand what to assess:

Defining what's expected
- 1a Mission, Vision, Values, Ethics, Role Models

Putting in place processes to get there
- 1b Develop & implement management systems

Engaging external parties
- 1c Interact with customers, partners & society

- 1e Identify & champion organizational change (Setting the tempo)
- 1d Communicate, motivate, and reinforce a culture of Excellence (Reinforcing behaviour)

For 1e you are analyzing how your leaders identify and champion organizational change

Leadership
Excellent leaders develop and facilitate the achievement of the mission and vision. They develop organizational values and systems required for sustainable success and implement these via their actions and behaviours. During periods of change they retain a constancy of purpose. Where required, such leaders are able to change the direction of the organization and inspire others to follow.

Step 2. Learn from what leaders in excellent organizations do for 1e:

They have leaders at all levels who build understanding of the internal and broader external issues affecting the organization and who are able to motivate employees to undertake the deployment of necessary change plans, this typically includes:

i. **Building awareness** of why the change is needed
ii. Creating **desire to support and participate** in the change
iii. **Developing knowledge** of how to change
iv. Fostering **ability to implement** new skills and behaviour
v. Providing **reinforcements to sustain** the change, including providing support to employees as they deal with change
vi. Consistently **monitoring and reviewing the effectiveness of changes** as they are made

APPENDIX 1: A SET OF X32 ANALYSIS PRO-FORMA'S

Steps 3-5: Analyze Key Activity-Behaviour for this Criterion-Part		
3: Approaches	4: Deployment	5: Assessment and Review
List the processes and behaviours that impact on this criterion part.	*To what extent do you intend to deploy each? Has this been effectively achieved?*	*How and how often do you review the effectiveness of each activity and the overall mix of approaches?*

Step 6: List the key actions and improvements that arose from the review activities you listed in step 5

Step 7: Conclude an analysis of your key strengths and areas for improvement for this Criterion-Part	
Strengths:	Areas for Improvement:

Step 8: Score your Analysis						
Approach:	%	Deployment:	%	Assessment & Review:	%	Overall:	%
Step 9: Tick one of the options to rank the strategic importance of addressing the issues arising from the analysis above						
☐ Not relevant	☐ Useful		☐ Important		☐ Critical to our success	

Policy and Strategy | 2a

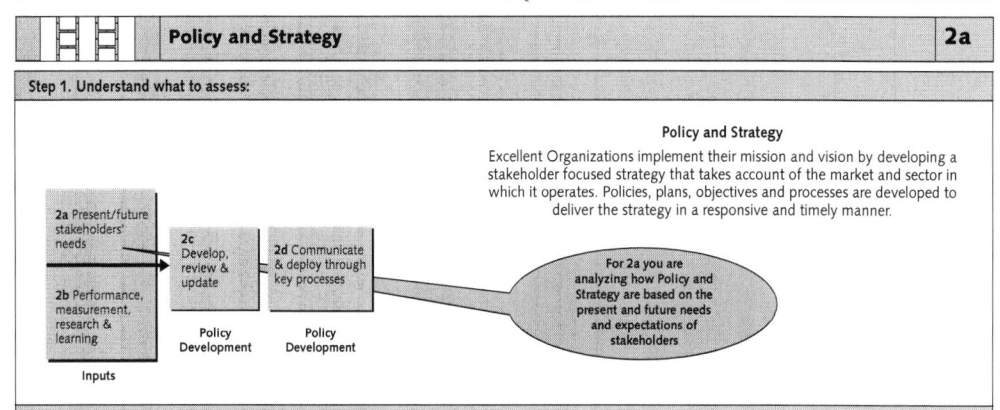

Step 1. Understand what to assess:

Policy and Strategy

Excellent Organizations implement their mission and vision by developing a stakeholder focused strategy that takes account of the market and sector in which it operates. Policies, plans, objectives and processes are developed to deliver the strategy in a responsive and timely manner.

- **2a** Present/future stakeholders' needs
- **2b** Performance, measurement, research & learning

Inputs

- **2c** Develop, review & update

Policy Development

- **2d** Communicate & deploy through key processes

Policy Development

For 2a you are analyzing how Policy and Strategy are based on the present and future needs and expectations of stakeholders

Step 2. Learn from what leaders in excellent organizations do for 2a:

They are effective at acquiring, analyzing, and disseminating relevant stakeholder focused information; this will typically include processes for:

i. Identifying and understanding the **needs of differing stakeholder groups** in a systematic way, for example, by defining individual executive responsibility for each

ii. **Meeting regularly with key stakeholders** in order to understand their ongoing needs;

iii. Closely tracking the competitive, environmental, societal, economic, and demographic **factors which may change stakeholder behaviour** in the market place (see also 2b)

iv. Anticipating the **impact of potential conflicts** resulting from the attempted balancing of the needs and priorities of different stakeholders

v. **Analyzing and agreeing** (for key stakeholders/partners), which **core business competence(s) will likely enable future success**, for example for customers by:
   o having a clear focus, and relevant data, on both existing and potential customers and their needs
   o carrying out research to find out why competitors' customers buy from them
   o seeking to understand the customer value chain in detail, and how it is likely to change in the future
   o analyzing responses such as above to conclude which business competences are 'core' to future success

APPENDIX 1: A SET OF X32 ANALYSIS PRO-FORMA'S

Steps 3-5: Analyze Key Activity-Behaviour for this Criterion-Part		
3: Approaches	4: Deployment	5: Assessment and Review
List the processes and behaviours that impact on this criterion part.	*To what extent do you intend to deploy each? Has this been effectively achieved?*	*How and how often do you review the effectiveness of each activity and the overall mix of approaches?*

Step 6: List the key actions and improvements that arose from the review activities you listed in step 5

Step 7: Conclude an analysis of your key strengths and areas for improvement for this Criterion-Part

Strengths:	Areas for Improvement:

Step 8: Score your Analysis

Approach: %	Deployment: %	Assessment & Review: %	Overall: %

Step 9: Tick one of the options to rank the strategic importance of addressing the issues arising from the analysis above

☐ Not relevant	☐ Useful	☐ Important	☐ Critical to our success

Policy and Strategy — 2b

Step 1. Understand what to assess:

Policy and Strategy

Excellent Organizations implement their mission and vision by developing a stakeholder focused strategy that takes account of the market and sector in which it operates. Policies, plans, objectives and processes are developed to deliver the strategy in a responsive and timely manner.

- 2a Present/future stakeholders' needs
- 2b Performance, measurement, research & learning
- 2c Develop, review & update
- 2d Communicate & deploy through key processes

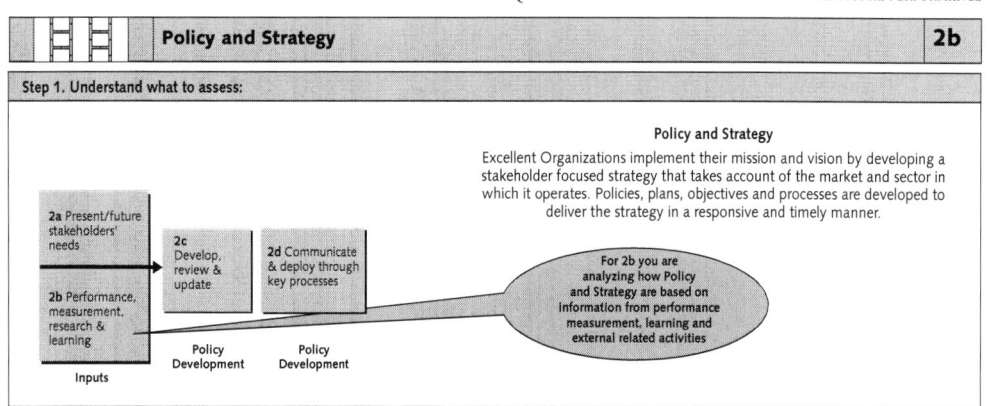

Inputs — Policy Development — Policy Development

For 2b you are analyzing how Policy and Strategy are based on information from performance measurement, learning and external related activities

Step 2. Learn from what leaders in excellent organizations do for 2b:

They have well structured processes for acquiring, analyzing, and disseminating relevant performance measurement, research and learning, seeking to identify strategic opportunities to gain through differentiated innovation, this will typically include:

i. Identifying and understanding the **key drivers** of organizational results
ii. Finding or developing data sources to **monitor, compare, benchmark and improve these drivers;**
iii. Analyzing and understanding the **historic performance of competitors**
iv. Identifying **and learning from relevant 'best in class' organizations**
v. Undertaking **market research**
vi. Understanding **brand and image** positioning
vii. Analyzing **micro and macroeconomic trends**
viii. Learning from evaluating **past business and product performance**
ix. Learning from **external networks or partnerships**
x. Identifying **political and regulatory issues**
xi. Assessing technological changes-innovations, looking for **disruptive market or technological practices**
xii. Identifying **social, environmental and cultural changes**

APPENDIX 1: A SET OF X32 ANALYSIS PRO-FORMA'S

Steps 3-5: Analyze Key Activity-Behaviour for this Criterion-Part		
3: Approaches	4: Deployment	5: Assessment and Review
List the processes and behaviours that impact on this criterion part.	*To what extent do you intend to deploy each? Has this been effectively achieved?*	*How and how often do you review the effectiveness of each activity and the overall mix of approaches?*

Step 6: List the key actions and improvements that arose from the review activities you listed in step 5

Step 7: Conclude an analysis of your key strengths and areas for improvement for this Criterion-Part

Strengths:	Areas for Improvement:

Step 8: Score your Analysis

Approach: %	Deployment: %	Assessment & Review: %	Overall: %

Step 9: Tick one of the options to rank the strategic importance of addressing the issues arising from the analysis above

☐ Not relevant	☐ Useful	☐ Important	☐ Critical to our success

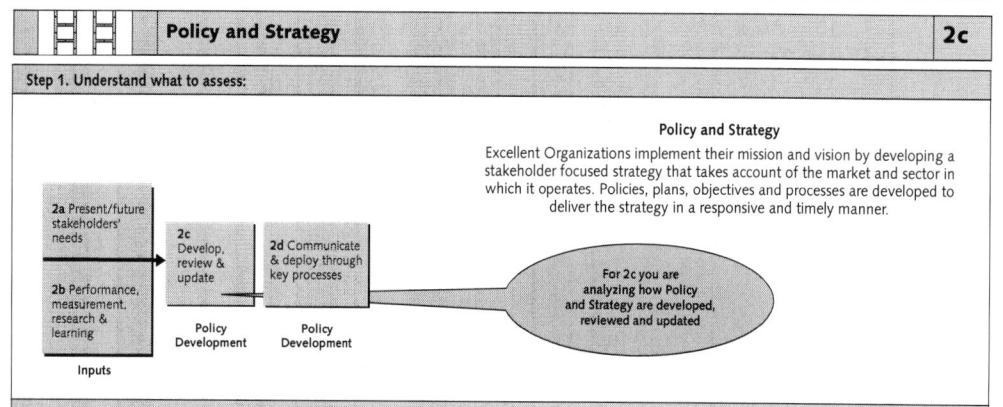

Policy and Strategy — 2c

Step 1. Understand what to assess:

Policy and Strategy

Excellent Organizations implement their mission and vision by developing a stakeholder focused strategy that takes account of the market and sector in which it operates. Policies, plans, objectives and processes are developed to deliver the strategy in a responsive and timely manner.

- **2a** Present/future stakeholders' needs
- **2b** Performance, measurement, research & learning

Inputs

- **2c** Develop, review & update — Policy Development
- **2d** Communicate & deploy through key processes — Policy Development

For 2c you are analyzing how Policy and Strategy are developed, reviewed and updated

Step 2. Learn from what leaders in excellent organizations do for 2c:

They use effective Policy and Strategy formulation-review approaches, informed by the data in 2a and 2b, these will typically include:

i. A well-defined **strategic management process**, operated through an annual or more frequent periodic planning cycle
ii. Structured methods to **review the effectiveness and relevance of past policy and strategy**, and the process used to develop it, on an annual basis, making use of benchmarking
iii. Ways to conclude the **key drivers** of stakeholder satisfaction and loyalty, and related core competencies of the organization-partners
iv. Ways to conclude **strategic and operational risks**
v. Processes by which to conclude **which market to address** and which to abandon
vi. Checks to ensure that policy and strategy are not overly biased by **external reporting requirements**;
vii. Recognizing that **speed and agility** are often critical factors for the future
viii. **Being prepared to challenge** any proposed plan where there is not agreement on how to measure its contribution to the agreed policy and strategy
ix. Seeking a balance between the pressures for maximizing short-term financial performance, and the need for long-term **sustainable growth**
x. Finding a manageable **balance** between the needs of all stakeholder groups

APPENDIX 1: A SET OF X32 ANALYSIS PRO-FORMA'S

Steps 3-5: Analyze Key Activity-Behaviour for this Criterion-Part		
3: Approaches	4: Deployment	5: Assessment and Review
List the processes and behaviours that impact on this criterion part.	*To what extent do you intend to deploy each? Has this been effectively achieved?*	*How and how often do you review the effectiveness of each activity and the overall mix of approaches?*

Step 6: List the key actions and improvements that arose from the review activities you listed in step 5

Step 7: Conclude an analysis of your key strengths and areas for improvement for this Criterion-Part

Strengths:	Areas for Improvement:

Step 8: Score your Analysis

Approach: %	Deployment: %	Assessment & Review: %	Overall: %

Step 9: Tick one of the options to rank the strategic importance of addressing the issues arising from the analysis above

☐ Not relevant	☐ Useful	☐ Important	☐ Critical to our success

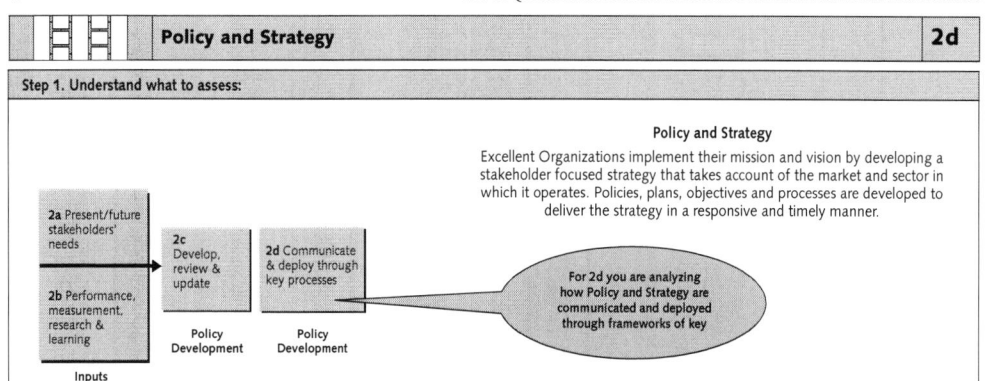

Policy and Strategy — 2d

Step 1. Understand what to assess:

Policy and Strategy

Excellent Organizations implement their mission and vision by developing a stakeholder focused strategy that takes account of the market and sector in which it operates. Policies, plans, objectives and processes are developed to deliver the strategy in a responsive and timely manner.

- **2a** Present/future stakeholders' needs
- **2b** Performance, measurement, research & learning

Inputs

- **2c** Develop, review & update — *Policy Development*
- **2d** Communicate & deploy through key processes — *Policy Development*

For 2d you are analyzing how Policy and Strategy are communicated and deployed through frameworks of key

Step 2. Learn from what leaders in excellent organizations do for 2d:

They have robust and pervasive methods for communication-deployment of Policy and Strategy; these will include processes for:

i. Defining and deploying a framework of **key processes** to deliver the organizations Policy and Strategy (see also 5a)
ii. Using **cross functional management forums, with multi level participation** to create the annual plans, formulate business unit strategies, design organizational structures (see also 3a) and develop and set organizational goals
iii. Ensuring that **performance measurement frameworks are aligned** with the organizations key processes/strategy, and are **not sub-optimized by functional boundaries or past-historic measurement practices**
iv. Reinforcing and making clear any **linkage or dependencies** between individual plans
v. **Aligning the boundaries of individual employee roles** to policy and strategy, so that effective empowerment is achieved (see also 3a/3c)
vi. Ensuring that **employees/other relevant stakeholders are aware** of policy and strategy and have clear targets for their performance/part in it
vii. Having systems to monitor variance to plan with **early warning flags** or indicators
viii. Establishing **timely and formal improvement plans if a performance indicator is below standard**

APPENDIX 1: A SET OF X32 ANALYSIS PRO-FORMA'S

Steps 3-5: Analyze Key Activity-Behaviour for this Criterion-Part

3: Approaches	4: Deployment	5: Assessment and Review
List the processes and behaviours that impact on this criterion part.	*To what extent do you intend to deploy each? Has this been effectively achieved?*	*How and how often do you review the effectiveness of each activity and the overall mix of approaches?*

Step 6: List the key actions and improvements that arose from the review activities you listed in step 5

Step 7: Conclude an analysis of your key strengths and areas for improvement for this Criterion-Part

Strengths:	Areas for Improvement:

Step 8: Score your Analysis

Approach: %	Deployment: %	Assessment & Review: %	Overall: %

Step 9: Tick one of the options to rank the strategic importance of addressing the issues arising from the analysis above

☐ Not relevant	☐ Useful	☐ Important	☐ Critical to our success

People Management — 3a

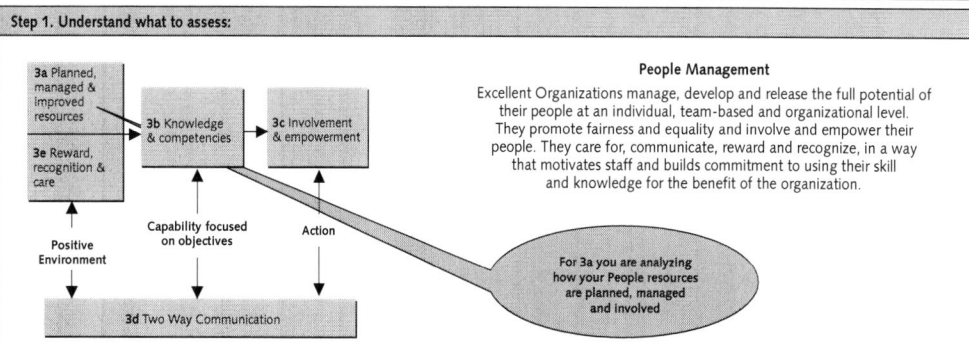

Step 1. Understand what to assess:

3a Planned, managed & improved resources
3b Knowledge & competencies
3c Involvement & empowerment
3e Reward, recognition & care
3d Two Way Communication

Positive Environment · Capability focused on objectives · Action

People Management
Excellent Organizations manage, develop and release the full potential of their people at an individual, team-based and organizational level. They promote fairness and equality and involve and empower their people. They care for, communicate, reward and recognize, in a way that motivates staff and builds commitment to using their skill and knowledge for the benefit of the organization.

For 3a you are analyzing how your People resources are planned, managed and involved

Step 2. Learn from what leaders in excellent organizations do for 3a:

They have strategically integrated methods for planning, managing and improving people resources, these will include:

i. Developing strategic people plans consistent with policy and strategy and with **capabilities to meet current, emerging and future business needs**
ii. **Designing-refining organizational structures** to align them with the organizations key processes, and increase the opportunity for ownership, clear workflows, and devolved decision-making
iii. **Aligning the boundaries of individual employee roles** to policy and strategy, so that effective empowerment is achieved (see also 2d, 3b, 3c)
iv. **Maintaining a monitor of employee-related measures**, including satisfaction, motivation, skills, safety, and well-being, and correlating this with the various indicators of organizational performance, in order to understand the contribution of people to success
v. Innovating with **recruitment based on defined, strategically aligned, competencies** and needs
vi. **Integrating line managers**, as well as HR professionals, in the recruitment and career development processes
vii. Using recruitment procedures at all levels, which **test attitude and motivation** as well as the core competence;
viii. Developing **partnerships with educational institutions-professional bodies** to ensure the future supply of well-prepared employees and educational support
ix. Having robust **succession plans for key posts**

APPENDIX 1: A SET OF X32 ANALYSIS PRO-FORMA'S

Steps 3-5: Analyze Key Activity-Behaviour for this Criterion-Part		
3: Approaches	4: Deployment	5: Assessment and Review
List the processes and behaviours that impact on this criterion part.	*To what extent do you intend to deploy each? Has this been effectively achieved?*	*How and how often do you review the effectiveness of each activity and the overall mix of approaches?*

Step 6: List the key actions and improvements that arose from the review activities you listed in step 5

Step 7: Conclude an analysis of your key strengths and areas for improvement for this Criterion-Part

Strengths:	Areas for Improvement:

Step 8: Score your Analysis

Approach: %	Deployment: %	Assessment & Review: %	Overall: %

Step 9: Tick one of the options to rank the strategic importance of addressing the issues arising from the analysis above

☐ Not relevant	☐ Useful	☐ Important	☐ Critical to our success

People Management — 3b

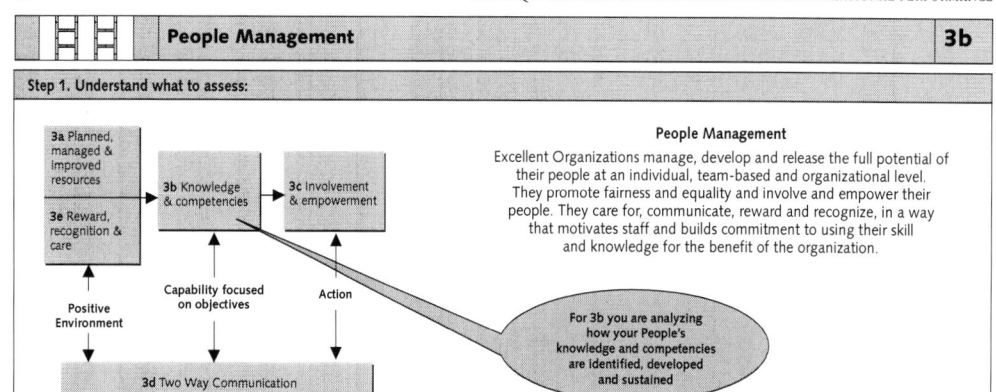

Step 1. Understand what to assess:

People Management

Excellent Organizations manage, develop and release the full potential of their people at an individual, team-based and organizational level. They promote fairness and equality and involve and empower their people. They care for, communicate, reward and recognize, in a way that motivates staff and builds commitment to using their skill and knowledge for the benefit of the organization.

Diagram showing:
- 3a Planned, managed & improved resources
- 3e Reward, recognition & care
- 3b Knowledge & competencies
- 3c Involvement & empowerment
- 3d Two Way Communication
- Positive Environment / Capability focused on objectives / Action

For 3b you are analyzing how your People's knowledge and competencies are identified, developed and sustained

Step 2. Learn from what leaders in excellent organizations do for 3b:

They use innovative methods to target, develop and sustain people knowledge and competencies, including:

i. **Involving** employees in developing strategies, plans and goals-objectives-targets
ii. **Aligning team and individual objectives** and targets with overall business goals in a structured way
iii. **Setting equitable goals and objectives** across all teams, recognising individuals and their levels of capability
iv. Having agreed objectives, targets and **development plans** for all employees
v. **Using coaching, counselling and support** when targets are not met, to agree, document and support an improvement plan
vi. Providing **structured opportunities** for people to enhance their competence and skills, ensuring that:
   - development **funds are budgeted**, prioritised and efficiently deployed
   - development is linked **to needs** identified in a structured **appraisal/personal development review** process
   - **innovative organizational and individual learning opportunities are created**, eg job rotation, presentations by customers, improvement teams, and visits by leaders from other organizations
   - training-development effectiveness is not only evaluated with post-event review forms, but also with **manager-led learning reviews**

APPENDIX 1: A SET OF X32 ANALYSIS PRO-FORMA'S

Steps 3-5: Analyze Key Activity-Behaviour for this Criterion-Part		
3: Approaches	4: Deployment	5: Assessment and Review
List the processes and behaviours that impact on this criterion part.	*To what extent do you intend to deploy each? Has this been effectively achieved?*	*How and how often do you review the effectiveness of each activity and the overall mix of approaches?*

Step 6: List the key actions and improvements that arose from the review activities you listed in step 5

Step 7: Conclude an analysis of your key strengths and areas for improvement for this Criterion-Part	
Strengths:	Areas for Improvement:

Step 8: Score your Analysis			
Approach: %	Deployment: %	Assessment & Review: %	Overall: %
Step 9: Tick one of the options to rank the strategic importance of addressing the issues arising from the analysis above			
☐ Not relevant	☐ Useful	☐ Important	☐ Critical to our success

People Management 3c

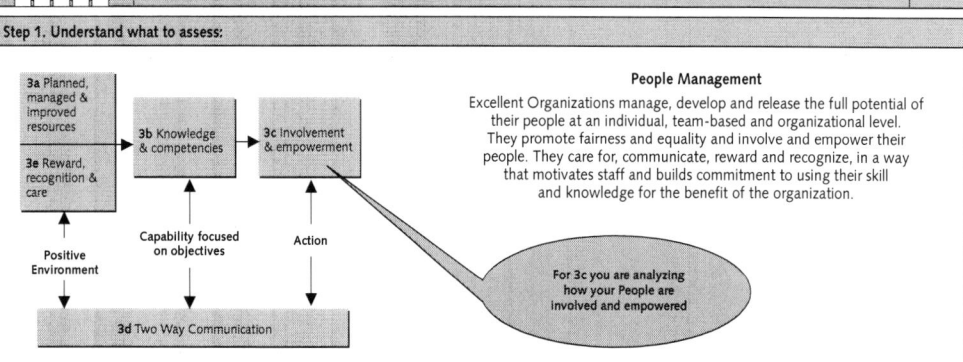

Step 1. Understand what to assess:

People Management

Excellent Organizations manage, develop and release the full potential of their people at an individual, team-based and organizational level. They promote fairness and equality and involve and empower their people. They care for, communicate, reward and recognize, in a way that motivates staff and builds commitment to using their skill and knowledge for the benefit of the organization.

For 3c you are analyzing how your People are involved and empowered

- 3a Planned, managed & improved resources
- 3e Reward, recognition & care
- 3b Knowledge & competencies
- 3c Involvement & empowerment
- 3d Two Way Communication

Positive Environment · Capability focused on objectives · Action

Step 2. Learn from what leaders in excellent organizations do for 3c:

They have strategically aligned methods for involving and empowering people and ensure that these:

i. Encourage people to **accept responsibility** for improving business performance and owning and solving their own problems, ensuring they feel valued and respected for their contribution
ii. Make **continuous improvement** of all products, processes and systems a formal goal for everyone
iii. Foster a spirit of experimentation, innovation, and creativity, **focusing on learning rather than blame**;
iv. **Delegate decisions**, but with the relevant information and support;
v. Encourage **free and informal sharing of information, knowledge and** experience between groups;
vi. Encourage involvement and **improvement contributions from both teams and individuals**;
vii. Have **processes to share best practice**, for example, improvement forums, road shows and in-house conferences
viii. Create **publications** to spread examples of improvement and best practice
ix. Maintain a **database of improvement solutions**;
x. Have mechanisms to encourage staff to **develop across different parts of the organization**, and so increase broad-based knowledge
xi. Set **clear boundaries** on what is not to be done

APPENDIX 1: A SET OF X32 ANALYSIS PRO-FORMA'S

Steps 3-5: Analyze Key Activity-Behaviour for this Criterion-Part		
3: Approaches	4: Deployment	5: Assessment and Review
List the processes and behaviours that impact on this criterion part.	*To what extent do you intend to deploy each? Has this been effectively achieved?*	*How and how often do you review the effectiveness of each activity and the overall mix of approaches?*

Step 6: List the key actions and improvements that arose from the review activities you listed in step 5

Step 7: Conclude an analysis of your key strengths and areas for improvement for this Criterion-Part	
Strengths:	Areas for Improvement:

Step 8: Score your Analysis			
Approach: %	Deployment: %	Assessment & Review: %	Overall: %
Step 9: Tick one of the options to rank the strategic importance of addressing the issues arising from the analysis above			
☐ Not relevant	☐ Useful	☐ Important	☐ Critical to our success

People Management — 3d

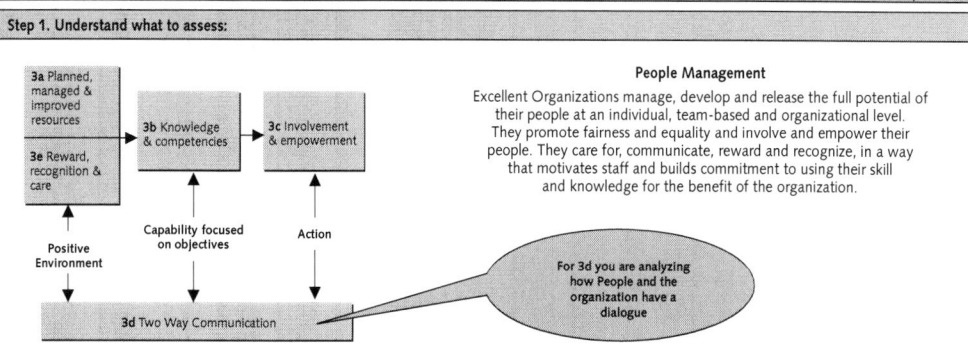

Step 1. Understand what to assess:

People Management

Excellent Organizations manage, develop and release the full potential of their people at an individual, team-based and organizational level. They promote fairness and equality and involve and empower their people. They care for, communicate, reward and recognize, in a way that motivates staff and builds commitment to using their skill and knowledge for the benefit of the organization.

- 3a Planned, managed & improved resources
- 3b Knowledge & competencies
- 3c Involvement & empowerment
- 3e Reward, recognition & care
- 3d Two Way Communication

Positive Environment — Capability focused on objectives — Action

For 3d you are analyzing how People and the organization have a dialogue

Step 2. Learn from what leaders in excellent organizations do for 3d:

They have aligned and effective communication and dialogue methods, and ensuring that these:

i. Systematically **identify the communication needs** of each part of the organization, and implement structured plans to satisfy them
ii. Identify and exploit the **communications channels** which employees say work best
iii. **Use straightforward language** which is free from jargon and management buzzwords
iv. **Address bottom-up and lateral dialogue** with the same emphasis given to top - down transmission
v. Are delivered by **presenters and briefers who are trained** and capable in running **two way** communication sessions
vi. Ensure **notice boards** are managed to avoid clutter and maintain focus
vii. Openly share both **good and bad** news
viii. Make sure that different teams **know what everyone else is doing**
ix. Ensure that everyone fully understands and **can communicate** the organizations purpose, objectives and plans
x. **Build understanding** of the need for new initiatives and other changes, by holding open discussions and allowing time for questions

APPENDIX 1: A SET OF X32 ANALYSIS PRO-FORMA'S

Steps 3-5: Analyze Key Activity-Behaviour for this Criterion-Part		
3: Approaches	4: Deployment	5: Assessment and Review
List the processes and behaviours that impact on this criterion part.	*To what extent do you intend to deploy each? Has this been effectively achieved?*	*How and how often do you review the effectiveness of each activity and the overall mix of approaches?*

Step 6: List the key actions and improvements that arose from the review activities you listed in step 5

Step 7: Conclude an analysis of your key strengths and areas for improvement for this Criterion-Part

Strengths:	Areas for Improvement:

Step 8: Score your Analysis

Approach: %	Deployment: %	Assessment & Review: %	Overall: %

Step 9: Tick one of the options to rank the strategic importance of addressing the issues arising from the analysis above

☐ Not relevant	☐ Useful	☐ Important	☐ Critical to our success

People Management — 3e

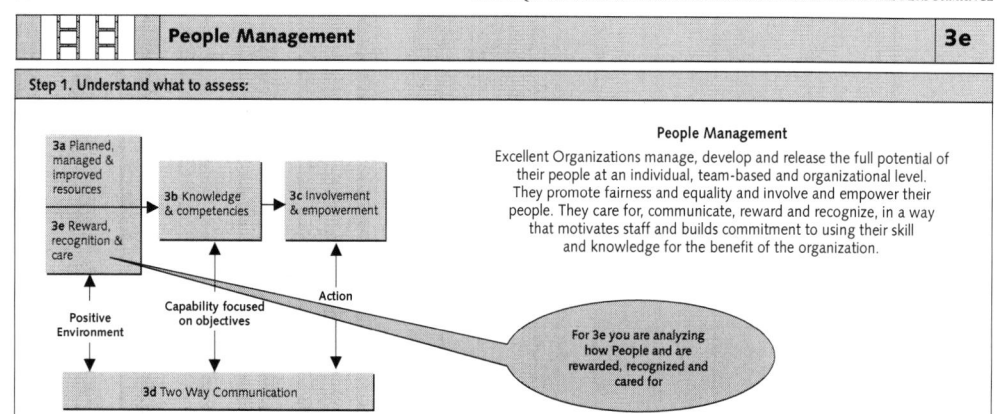

Step 1. Understand what to assess:

3a Planned, managed & improved resources
3b Knowledge & competencies
3c Involvement & empowerment
3e Reward, recognition & care
3d Two Way Communication

Positive Environment
Capability focused on objectives
Action

People Management
Excellent Organizations manage, develop and release the full potential of their people at an individual, team-based and organizational level. They promote fairness and equality and involve and empower their people. They care for, communicate, reward and recognize, in a way that motivates staff and builds commitment to using their skill and knowledge for the benefit of the organization.

For 3e you are analyzing how People and are rewarded, recognized and cared for

Step 2. Learn from what leaders in excellent organizations do for 3e:

They have reward, recognition and care processes that ensure:

i. People feel **valued for their contribution**
ii. They are **motivated to individual and collective actions that improve business results**
iii. Consistent organization-wide principles are used to ensure **fair rating of individuals or teams**
iv. Employee needs and preferences are understood and based on those preferences **a mix of supportive reward-recognition practices** are promoted, including:
   - structured **remuneration, redeployment and redundancy methods**
   - structured **recognition processes** (eg thank-you's, awards/prizes, etc.)
   - **ancillary benefits** (potentially including: social and cultural activity support, job sharing, career breaks, tele-working, flexible hours, childcare provision, independent financial planning-pensions, provision of social, cultural and health-environment training and such like)

APPENDIX 1: A SET OF X32 ANALYSIS PRO-FORMA'S

Steps 3-5: Analyze Key Activity-Behaviour for this Criterion-Part			
3: Approaches	4: Deployment		5: Assessment and Review
List the processes and behaviours that impact on this criterion part.	*To what extent do you intend to deploy each? Has this been effectively achieved?*		*How and how often do you review the effectiveness of each activity and the overall mix of approaches?*
Step 6: List the key actions and improvements that arose from the review activities you listed in step 5			
Step 7: Conclude an analysis of your key strengths and areas for improvement for this Criterion-Part			
Strengths:		Areas for Improvement:	
Step 8: Score your Analysis			
Approach: %	Deployment: %	Assessment & Review: %	Overall: %
Step 9: Tick one of the options to rank the strategic importance of addressing the issues arising from the analysis above			
☐ Not relevant	☐ Useful	☐ Important	☐ Critical to our success

Partnership and Resource Management | 4a

Step 1. Understand what to assess:

- 4a External Partnerships — Alignment
- 4b Finances — Alignment
- 4c Buildings, equipment and materials — Alignment
- 4d Technology — Alignment
- 4e Information & Knowledge — Alignment

→ Criterion 2 Policy & Strategy

Partnerships and Resources

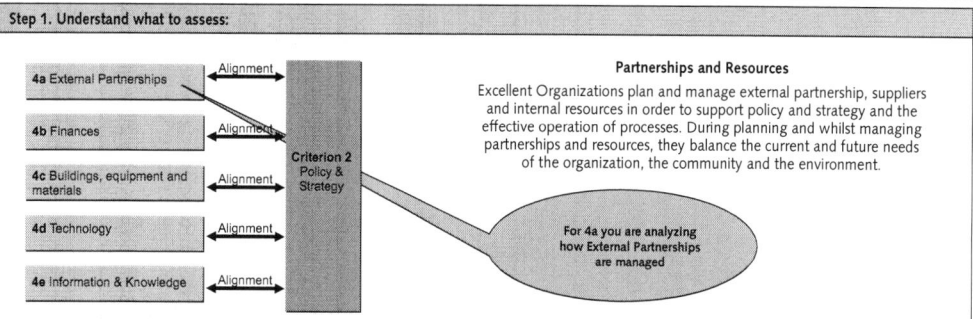

Excellent Organizations plan and manage external partnership, suppliers and internal resources in order to support policy and strategy and the effective operation of processes. During planning and whilst managing partnerships and resources, they balance the current and future needs of the organization, the community and the environment.

For 4a you are analyzing how External Partnerships are managed

Step 2. Learn from what leaders in excellent organizations do for 4a:

They work collaboratively with business partners/suppliers to improve added-value in the supply chain; typically this includes:

i. **Defining key partners/strategic suppliers** and contractors and developing effective relationships at executive levels
ii. Conducting regular and systematic **reviews of the relationship** with key suppliers
iii. Sponsoring and resourcing **joint improvement activity with partners**, in order to improve the quality of products or services, and to build core competencies and capability for the future
iv. Assessing and developing the **environmental performance** of suppliers and **balancing short-term gain with long-term** considerations for both the organizations and society at large
v. Documenting partner supplier performance and **jointly agreeing improvement targets**
vi. **Setting contractual targets for the capability** of suppliers' processes
vii. **Sharing information** with suppliers and partners, and operating in an environment of mutual benefit
viii. **Presenting awards** to suppliers/partners to recognize improvements
ix. Integrating partners with the organizations **key processes** by, for example, line side delivery of key parts, or 'implants' of supplier staff within the organization
x. **Utilising the expertise** of suppliers and partners in the design of new products and facilities
xi. Aspiring to developing **partnership relationships** with statutory bodies, industry regulators and enforcement services within the community

APPENDIX 1: A SET OF X32 ANALYSIS PRO-FORMA'S

Steps 3-5: Analyze Key Activity-Behaviour for this Criterion-Part		
3: Approaches	4: Deployment	5: Assessment and Review
List the processes and behaviours that impact on this criterion part.	*To what extent do you intend to deploy each? Has this been effectively achieved?*	*How and how often do you review the effectiveness of each activity and the overall mix of approaches?*

Step 6: List the key actions and improvements that arose from the review activities you listed in step 5

Step 7: Conclude an analysis of your key strengths and areas for improvement for this Criterion-Part

Strengths:	Areas for Improvement:

Step 8: Score your Analysis

Approach: %	Deployment: %	Assessment & Review: %	Overall: %

Step 9: Tick one of the options to rank the strategic importance of addressing the issues arising from the analysis above

☐ Not relevant	☐ Useful	☐ Important	☐ Critical to our success

Partnership and Resource Management — 4b

Step 1. Understand what to assess:

- **4a** External Partnerships — Alignment
- **4b** Finances — Alignment
- **4c** Buildings, equipment and materials — Alignment
- **4d** Technology — Alignment
- **4e** Information & Knowledge — Alignment

→ Criterion 2 Policy & Strategy

Partnerships and Resources

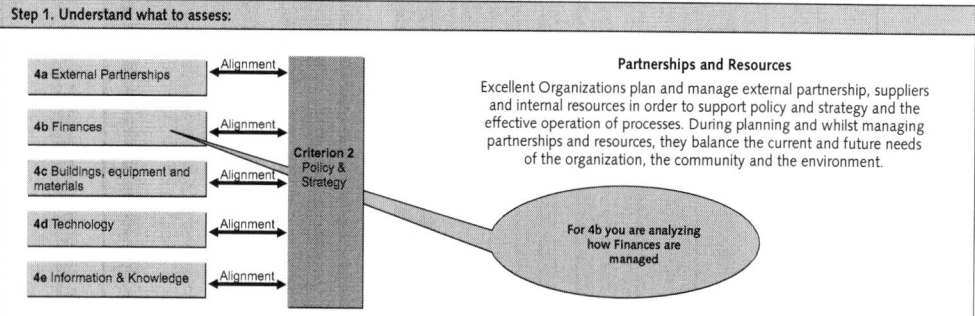

Excellent Organizations plan and manage external partnership, suppliers and internal resources in order to support policy and strategy and the effective operation of processes. During planning and whilst managing partnerships and resources, they balance the current and future needs of the organization, the community and the environment.

For 4b you are analyzing how Finances are managed

Step 2. Learn from what leaders in excellent organizations do for 4b:

They optimize the provision/management of financial resources in support of the strategic growth of the organization, this includes:

i. Understanding the **financing needs of current and future strategies** and obtaining the finance for growth
ii. Ensuring that external controls on financial flexibility are managed to balance the need for **ethical and transparent governance** with maximum freedom to operate within the organization
iii. Managing **currency and other financial risks**
iv. **Integrating** financial management and operational-planning systems
v. Understanding and enhancing the **value of both tangible and intangible assets**
vi. Planning and reviewing every **capital investment** for delivery of expected benefits
vii. Using a consistent and systematic, formal approach to **project management**
viii. Simultaneously **measuring projects** by progress-to-plan, spend-to-plan and benefits-to-plan
ix. Ensuring that employees are aware of the **financial cost** of all materials used in the organization and accept the role of optimising such expenditure by focusing on **eliminating waste** of all kinds
x. Having strategically focused and **efficient financial reporting mechanisms**

APPENDIX 1: A SET OF X32 ANALYSIS PRO-FORMA'S

Steps 3-5: Analyze Key Activity-Behaviour for this Criterion-Part		
3: Approaches	4: Deployment	5: Assessment and Review
List the processes and behaviours that impact on this criterion part.	*To what extent do you intend to deploy each? Has this been effectively achieved?*	*How and how often do you review the effectiveness of each activity and the overall mix of approaches?*

Step 6: List the key actions and improvements that arose from the review activities you listed in step 5

Step 7: Conclude an analysis of your key strengths and areas for improvement for this Criterion-Part	
Strengths:	Areas for Improvement:

Step 8: Score your Analysis

Approach:	%	Deployment:	%	Assessment & Review:	%	Overall:	%

Step 9: Tick one of the options to rank the strategic importance of addressing the issues arising from the analysis above			
☐ Not relevant	☐ Useful	☐ Important	☐ Critical to our success

Partnership and Resource Management — 4c

Step 1. Understand what to assess:

- 4a External Partnerships — Alignment
- 4b Finances — Alignment
- 4c Buildings, equipment and materials — Alignment
- 4d Technology — Alignment
- 4e Information & Knowledge — Alignment

Criterion 2 Policy & Strategy

Partnerships and Resources
Excellent Organizations plan and manage external partnership, suppliers and internal resources in order to support policy and strategy and the effective operation of processes. During planning and whilst managing partnerships and resources, they balance the current and future needs of the organization, the community and the environment.

For 4c you are analyzing how buildings, equipment and materials are managed

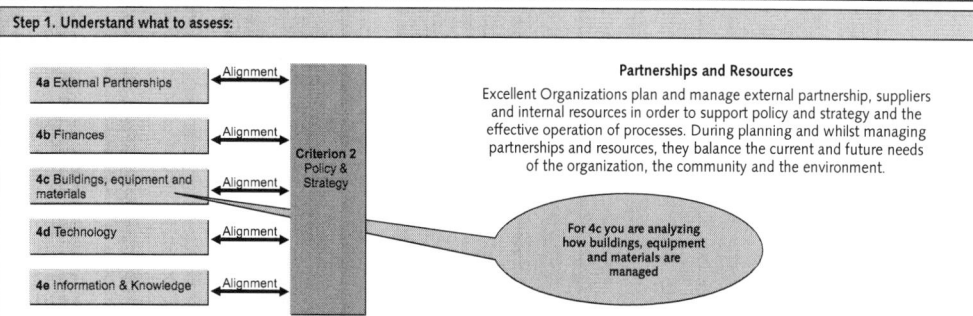

Step 2. Learn from what leaders in excellent organizations do for 4c:

They optimize the management of buildings, equipment and materials in support of the growth of the organization; this will include:

i. Managing building and **planning needs linked to future strategic growth**
ii. Adopting appropriate **preventative maintenance strategies**, based on the strategic role of each building
iii. Carrying out **environmental impact assessments**
iv. Reviewing the **use of space** for efficiency, ergonomics, access, storage, and visible control
v. **Regularly reviewing** the use of materials, work in progress and inventory
vi. Regularly reviewing **asset registers** and clearing out obsolete equipment
vii. Designing the **workplace layout** to foster employee interaction and innovation
viii. Optimising **transport usage**
ix. Encouraging waste reduction, **recycling and energy minimisation** activities
x. Ensuring that the **impact of fixed assets** and materials on the company/community/ employees is assessed
xi. Systematically measuring and reviewing the **performance and capacity of key physical assets**, for example, major production equipment
xii. Working with **utilities providers** to minimise energy cost and loss
xiii. Developing **major incident plans** with emergency services organizations to ensure community and employee safety, and testing and reviewing these at regular intervals

APPENDIX 1: A SET OF X32 ANALYSIS PRO-FORMA'S

Steps 3-5: Analyze Key Activity-Behaviour for this Criterion-Part

3: Approaches	4: Deployment	5: Assessment and Review
List the processes and behaviours that impact on this criterion part.	*To what extent do you intend to deploy each? Has this been effectively achieved?*	*How and how often do you review the effectiveness of each activity and the overall mix of approaches?*

Step 6: List the key actions and improvements that arose from the review activities you listed in step 5

Step 7: Conclude an analysis of your key strengths and areas for improvement for this Criterion-Part

Strengths:	Areas for Improvement:

Step 8: Score your Analysis

Approach: %	Deployment: %	Assessment & Review: %	Overall: %

Step 9: Tick one of the options to rank the strategic importance of addressing the issues arising from the analysis above

☐ Not relevant	☐ Useful	☐ Important	☐ Critical to our success

Partnership and Resource Management — 4d

Step 1. Understand what to assess:

- 4a External Partnerships — Alignment
- 4b Finances — Alignment
- 4c Buildings, equipment and materials — Alignment
- 4d Technology — Alignment
- 4e Information & Knowledge — Alignment

→ Criterion 2 Policy & Strategy

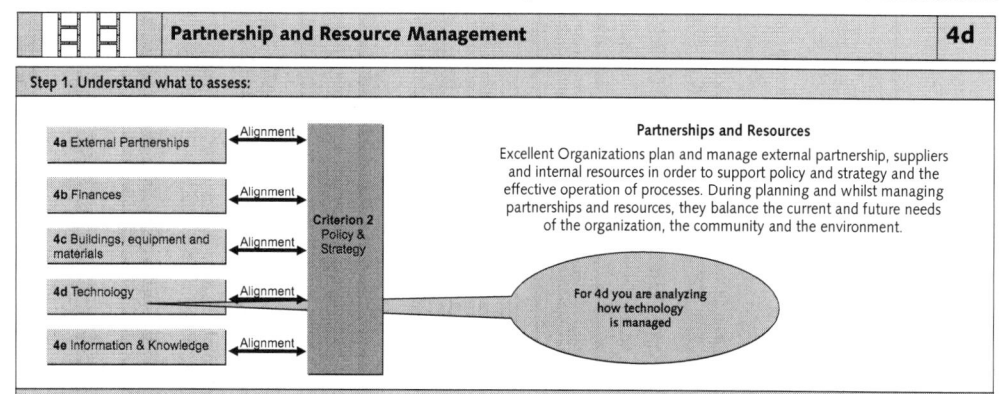

Partnerships and Resources

Excellent Organizations plan and manage external partnership, suppliers and internal resources in order to support policy and strategy and the effective operation of processes. During planning and whilst managing partnerships and resources, they balance the current and future needs of the organization, the community and the environment.

For 4d you are analyzing how technology is managed

Step 2. Learn from what leaders in excellent organizations do for 4d:

They optimise the management of technology in support of the strategic growth of the organization; this typically includes:

i. Tracking, evaluating and integrating the **latest trends in technology**
ii. Concluding the **technology enablers of strategy**
iii. Ensuring that the needed skills and capabilities of people are identified, developed and improved in **advance of developing technology**
iv. Adopting **scenario planning** techniques to assess future opportunities, risks and potentially disruptive technologies, and then engaging key managers in the scenarios in order to ensure employee preparedness and learning
v. Evaluating **patents and innovations of competitors**
vi. Spotting **fast moving market changes**
vii. **Intellectual property protection/patent** filing processes
viii. Rewarding or recognising employees for inventions which become **patentable**
ix. **Managing obsolescence** of current technologies

APPENDIX 1: A SET OF X32 ANALYSIS PRO-FORMA'S

Steps 3-5: Analyze Key Activity-Behaviour for this Criterion-Part		
3: Approaches	**4: Deployment**	**5: Assessment and Review**
List the processes and behaviours that impact on this criterion part.	*To what extent do you intend to deploy each? Has this been effectively achieved?*	*How and how often do you review the effectiveness of each activity and the overall mix of approaches?*

Step 6: List the key actions and improvements that arose from the review activities you listed in step 5

Step 7: Conclude an analysis of your key strengths and areas for improvement for this Criterion-Part

Strengths:	Areas for Improvement:

Step 8: Score your Analysis

Approach: %	Deployment: %	Assessment & Review: %	Overall: %

Step 9: Tick one of the options to rank the strategic importance of addressing the issues arising from the analysis above

☐ Not relevant	☐ Useful	☐ Important	☐ Critical to our success

Partnership and Resource Management — 4e

Step 1. Understand what to assess:

- 4a External Partnerships — Alignment
- 4b Finances — Alignment
- 4c Buildings, equipment and materials — Alignment
- 4d Technology — Alignment
- 4e Information & Knowledge — Alignment

→ Criterion 2 Policy & Strategy

Partnerships and Resources

Excellent Organizations plan and manage external partnership, suppliers and internal resources in order to support policy and strategy and the effective operation of processes. During planning and whilst managing partnerships and resources, they balance the current and future needs of the organization, the community and the environment.

For 4e you are analyzing how information and Knowledge are managed

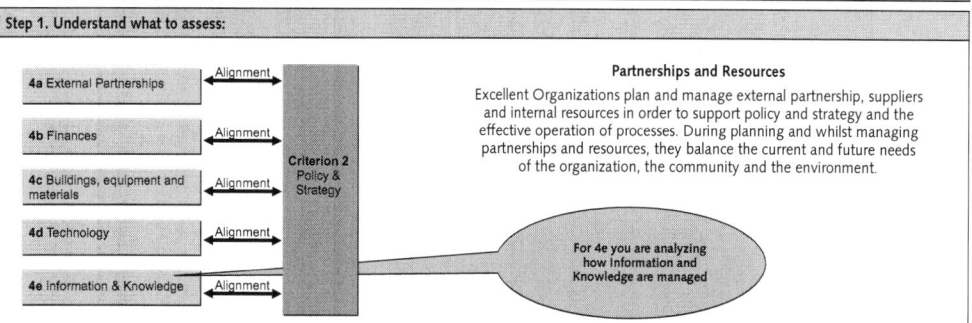

Step 2. Learn from what leaders in excellent organizations do for 4e:

They optimise the management of information and knowledge in support of the growth of the organization, this typically includes:

i. Creating an **Knowledge strategy** that supports the organizations Policy and Strategy
ii. Creating an **IT strategy**, which targets and delivers planned levels of people access, inter-system access, and appropriate levels of validity and security for key knowledge
iii. Achieving **appropriate integration** of multiple IT operating systems and knowledge sources
iv. Measuring and acting to improve the **effectiveness and user satisfaction with IT service provision**
v. Having ways to evaluate and **use information as a source of competitive advantage** (eg communities of practice to evaluate and make 'connections')
vi. Using **creativity and other tools** to make connections within the available knowledge
vii. Using systematic Knowledge transfer processes **to Share knowledge**, including with partner organizations
viii. **Intellectual property protection/patent filing** processes

APPENDIX 1: A SET OF X32 ANALYSIS PRO-FORMA'S

Steps 3-5: Analyze Key Activity-Behaviour for this Criterion-Part		
3: Approaches	4: Deployment	5: Assessment and Review
List the processes and behaviours that impact on this criterion part.	*To what extent do you intend to deploy each? Has this been effectively achieved?*	*How and how often do you review the effectiveness of each activity and the overall mix of approaches?*

Step 6: List the key actions and improvements that arose from the review activities you listed in step 5

Step 7: Conclude an analysis of your key strengths and areas for improvement for this Criterion-Part

Strengths:	Areas for Improvement:

Step 8: Score your Analysis

Approach: %	Deployment: %	Assessment & Review: %	Overall: %

Step 9: Tick one of the options to rank the strategic importance of addressing the issues arising from the analysis above

☐ Not relevant	☐ Useful	☐ Important	☐ Critical to our success

Process Management — 5a

Step 1. Understand what to assess:

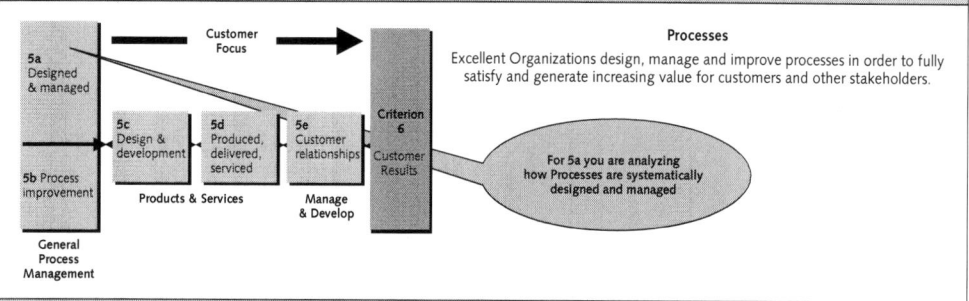

Processes
Excellent Organizations design, manage and improve processes in order to fully satisfy and generate increasing value for customers and other stakeholders.

For 5a you are analyzing how Processes are systematically designed and managed

- 5a Designed & managed
- 5b Process improvement
- General Process Management
- 5c Design & development
- 5d Produced, delivered, serviced
- 5e Customer relationships
- Products & Services
- Manage & Develop
- Customer Focus
- Criterion 6 Customer Results

Step 2. Learn from what leaders in excellent organizations do for 5a:

They have effective methods for designing and managing the value of the processes they use; this will include:

i. An approach to designing/reviewing the **key processes** needed to deliver Policy and Strategy
ii. **Involving key partners** in process thinking, identification, and design
iii. Creating **high-level process maps** to describe the structure of, and linkages between, all the key processes, other operational practices and how they add value aligned with the organizations aims/strategy
iv. Evaluating the detailed **impact of every process** on the organizations Policy and Strategy
v. **Identifying owners** for each whole process and sub-processes
vi. Defining **operating standards** for processes, and using such standards as the basis for internal/external audits;
vii. Ensuring that systematic and **valid methods are used to gather reliable data** on process performance;
viii. Using benchmarking, statistical variation/ process capability data, and process validation studies, to **identify, prioritise, and set targets for improvement;**
ix. Establishing clear goals for **process innovation**
x. **Systematically reviewing** each activity, at the key process level, to check performance against defined measures and targets

APPENDIX 1: A SET OF X32 ANALYSIS PRO-FORMA'S

Steps 3-5: Analyze Key Activity-Behaviour for this Criterion-Part

3: Approaches	4: Deployment	5: Assessment and Review
List the processes and behaviours that impact on this criterion part.	*To what extent do you intend to deploy each? Has this been effectively achieved?*	*How and how often do you review the effectiveness of each activity and the overall mix of approaches?*

Step 6: List the key actions and improvements that arose from the review activities you listed in step 5

Step 7: Conclude an analysis of your key strengths and areas for improvement for this Criterion-Part

Strengths:	Areas for Improvement:

Step 8: Score your Analysis

Approach: %	Deployment: %	Assessment & Review: %	Overall: %

Step 9: Tick one of the options to rank the strategic importance of addressing the issues arising from the analysis above

☐ Not relevant	☐ Useful	☐ Important	☐ Critical to our success

Process Management — 5b

Step 1. Understand what to assess:

Processes

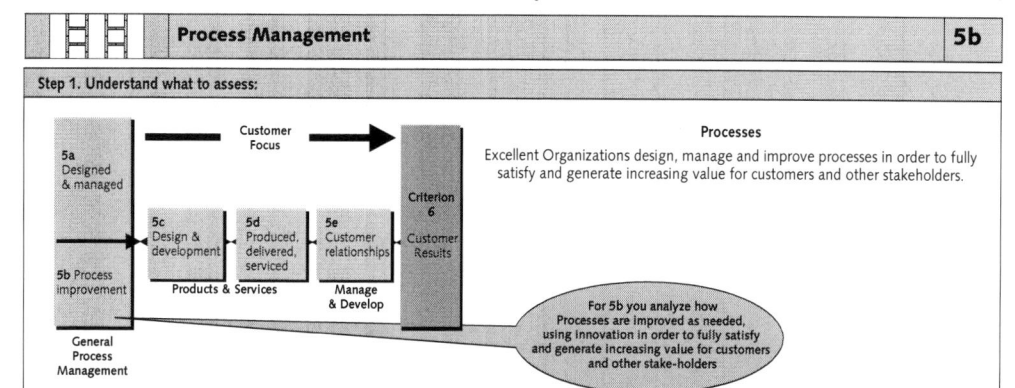

Excellent Organizations design, manage and improve processes in order to fully satisfy and generate increasing value for customers and other stakeholders.

For 5b you analyze how Processes are improved as needed, using innovation in order to fully satisfy and generate increasing value for customers and other stake-holders

Step 2. Learn from what leaders in excellent organizations do for 5b:

They have effective methods for innovating and improving the processes they use. This will typically include:

i. **Using the views** of customers, suppliers, auditors, and other stakeholders, along with process measurement to stimulate creativity in process management and improvement, and to identify improvement priorities
ii. **Developing a common approach** to improvement across these stakeholder groups
iii. Using benchmarking, statistical variation/process capability data and process validation studies, to **identify, prioritize and set targets for improvement**
iv. Carrying out **simple risk assessments** before piloting new ideas
v. **Piloting** the use of new techniques and operating philosophies, and evaluating the benefits carefully against pre-set requirements before adopting them
vi. Considering **employee training** as an integral part of their process change-introduction plan
vii. Using **feedback systems to capture lessons learned**, and apply these for further improvement
viii. Evaluating all changes for their **impact on top-level performance measures**, and use this to review the effectiveness of a changed process

APPENDIX 1: A SET OF X32 ANALYSIS PRO-FORMA'S

Steps 3-5: Analyze Key Activity-Behaviour for this Criterion-Part		
3: Approaches	4: Deployment	5: Assessment and Review
List the processes and behaviours that impact on this criterion part.	*To what extent do you intend to deploy each? Has this been effectively achieved?*	*How and how often do you review the effectiveness of each activity and the overall mix of approaches?*

Step 6: List the key actions and improvements that arose from the review activities you listed in step 5

Step 7: Conclude an analysis of your key strengths and areas for improvement for this Criterion-Part	
Strengths:	Areas for Improvement:

Step 8: Score your Analysis			
Approach: %	Deployment: %	Assessment & Review: %	Overall: %
Step 9: Tick one of the options to rank the strategic importance of addressing the issues arising from the analysis above			
☐ Not relevant	☐ Useful	☐ Important	☐ Critical to our success

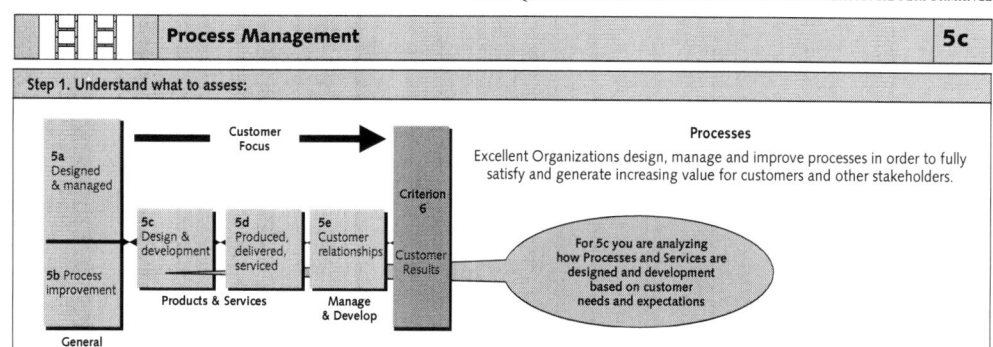

Process Management 5c

Step 1. Understand what to assess:

Processes

Excellent Organizations design, manage and improve processes in order to fully satisfy and generate increasing value for customers and other stakeholders.

For 5c you are analyzing how Processes and Services are designed and development based on customer needs and expectations

Step 2. Learn from what leaders in excellent organizations do for 5c:

They use structured methods for designing and developing a portfolio of new products and services based on customer needs and expectations. This will typically include:

i. **Using market research and soliciting customer input** throughout all stages of the product life cycle to ensure ongoing satisfaction as well as to identify ideas for new or improved products and services.
ii. Monitoring **competitive offerings**.
iii. Understanding the relevance of **technological changes** for products (see also 4d)
iv. Determining the **potential deficiencies of current products and services**
v. Identifying **innovations that meet customers' needs and wants,** engaging key partners and other stakeholders to help as appropriate
vi. Developing a **new product or service concept**
vii. Managing **the realization project** with cost, quality, environmental and delivery targets and **lifecycle planning**
viii. **Systematically reviewing** each development activity to check performance against defined measures and targets

APPENDIX 1: A SET OF X32 ANALYSIS PRO-FORMA'S

Steps 3-5: Analyze Key Activity-Behaviour for this Criterion-Part		
3: Approaches	4: Deployment	5: Assessment and Review
List the processes and behaviours that impact on this criterion part.	*To what extent do you intend to deploy each? Has this been effectively achieved?*	*How and how often do you review the effectiveness of each activity and the overall mix of approaches?*

Step 6: List the key actions and improvements that arose from the review activities you listed in step 5

Step 7: Conclude an analysis of your key strengths and areas for improvement for this Criterion-Part

Strengths:	Areas for Improvement:

Step 8: Score your Analysis

Approach: %	Deployment: %	Assessment & Review: %	Overall: %

Step 9: Tick one of the options to rank the strategic importance of addressing the issues arising from the analysis above

☐ Not relevant	☐ Useful	☐ Important	☐ Critical to our success

Process Management — 5d

Step 1. Understand what to assess:

Processes

Excellent Organizations design, manage and improve processes in order to fully satisfy and generate increasing value for customers and other stakeholders.

For 5d you are analyzing how Products and Services are produced, delivered and serviced

Diagram elements:
- 5a Designed & managed
- 5b Process improvement
- 5c Design & development
- 5d Produced, delivered, serviced
- 5e Customer relationships
- Products & Services
- Manage & Develop
- Customer Focus → Criterion 6 Customer Results

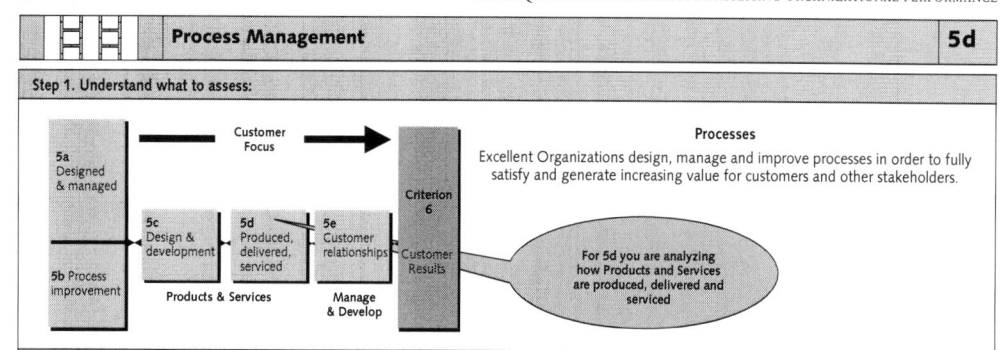

Step 2. Learn from what leaders in excellent organizations do for 5d:

They structure workflow, schedules and resource allocation to ensure effective product/service production, delivery and servicing. -This is very specific to an organization and its products-services, but can include:

i. Identifying target market segments
ii. Selecting channels of distribution
iii. Maintaining pricing strategies and value propositions
iv. Developing advertising and promotion strategies
v. Developing sales forecast
vi. Establishing presence in emerging markets
vii. Selling to customers through a field sales force
viii. Selling to customers through retail operations
ix. Selling to customers through the Internet
x. Selling to customers through direct marketing
xi. Managing wholesalers, retailers, and distributors
xii. Managing customer orders
xiii. Planning/acquiring necessary production resources
xiv. Converting resources into products/services
xv. Moving materials and resources
xvi. Packaging product
xvii. Warehousing or storing products
xviii. Managing inventories
xix. Managing delivery process
xx. Assuring product quality
xxi. Scheduling and performing maintenance
xxii. Monitor environmental, health, and safety performance
xxiii. Customer billing
xxiv. Responding to billing inquiries
xxv. Eliminating quality and reliability problems
xxvi. Eliminating outdated products and services

APPENDIX 1: A SET OF X32 ANALYSIS PRO-FORMA'S

Steps 3-5: Analyze Key Activity-Behaviour for this Criterion-Part		
3: Approaches	4: Deployment	5: Assessment and Review
List the processes and behaviours that impact on this criterion part.	*To what extent do you intend to deploy each? Has this been effectively achieved?*	*How and how often do you review the effectiveness of each activity and the overall mix of approaches?*

Step 6: List the key actions and improvements that arose from the review activities you listed in step 5

Step 7: Conclude an analysis of your key strengths and areas for improvement for this Criterion-Part

Strengths:	Areas for Improvement:

Step 8: Score your Analysis

Approach: %	Deployment: %	Assessment & Review: %	Overall: %

Step 9: Tick one of the options to rank the strategic importance of addressing the issues arising from the analysis above

☐ Not relevant	☐ Useful	☐ Important	☐ Critical to our success

Process Management — 5e

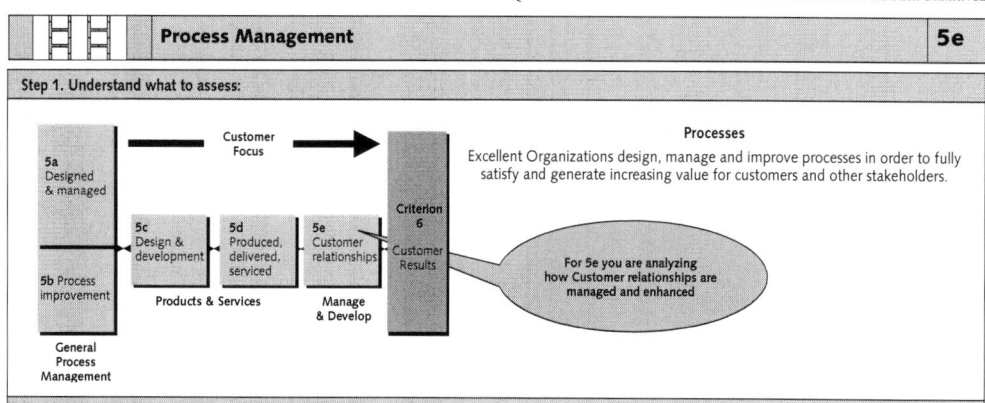

Step 1. Understand what to assess:

Processes
Excellent Organizations design, manage and improve processes in order to fully satisfy and generate increasing value for customers and other stakeholders.

For 5e you are analyzing how Customer relationships are managed and enhanced

- 5a Designed & managed
- 5b Process improvement
- General Process Management
- 5c Design & development
- 5d Produced, delivered, serviced
- Products & Services
- 5e Customer relationships — Manage & Develop
- Customer Focus → Criterion 6 Customer Results

Step 2. Learn from what leaders in excellent organizations do for 5e:

They have effective methods for managing the customer relations. This will typically include structured approaches to:

i. Having a clear understanding of the **customer base and the organization's priorities** in serving it
ii. Ensuring that their **staff are aware of end-users,** and how they value the product or service
iii. **Communicating key customer information and performance data,** so that all involved understand the nature of the relationships, and are motivated to respond
iv. Gathering, analyzing and **acting on feedback** from existing customers
v. **Analyzing the reasons** for losing existing customers and gaining new ones
vi. Investigating why some potential customers **only do business with their competitors**
vii. Using an **independent third party** data source to gather an unbiased view of customer perceptions
viii. Understanding **what the customer values** in the product or service
ix. Monitoring and **validating customer preference** data
x. Monitoring and **anticipating emerging customer and market needs**
xi. **Collaborating** with customers
xii. **Educating customers,** for example on the effective and responsible use of the provided product

Steps 3-5: Analyze Key Activity-Behaviour for this Criterion-Part

3: Approaches	4: Deployment	5: Assessment and Review
List the processes and behaviours that impact on this criterion part.	*To what extent do you intend to deploy each? Has this been effectively achieved?*	*How and how often do you review the effectiveness of each activity and the overall mix of approaches?*

Step 6: List the key actions and improvements that arose from the review activities you listed in step 5

Step 7: Conclude an analysis of your key strengths and areas for improvement for this Criterion-Part

Strengths:	Areas for Improvement:

Step 8: Score your Analysis

Approach: %	Deployment: %	Assessment & Review: %	Overall: %

Step 9: Tick one of the options to rank the strategic importance of addressing the issues arising from the analysis above

☐ Not relevant	☐ Useful	☐ Important	☐ Critical to our success

Customer Results | 6a

Step 1. Understand what to assess:

6b Performance Indicators
Internal measures
Performance Drivers

→

6a Perception Measures
Customer views
Feedback From the Stakeholder

Customer Results
Excellent Organizations comprehensively measure and achieve outstanding results with respect to Customers.

Excellent organizations understand what is key to measure to understand and influence both customer results and the achievement of their strategies.

For 6a you are analyzing **Customer Perceptions** of the organization

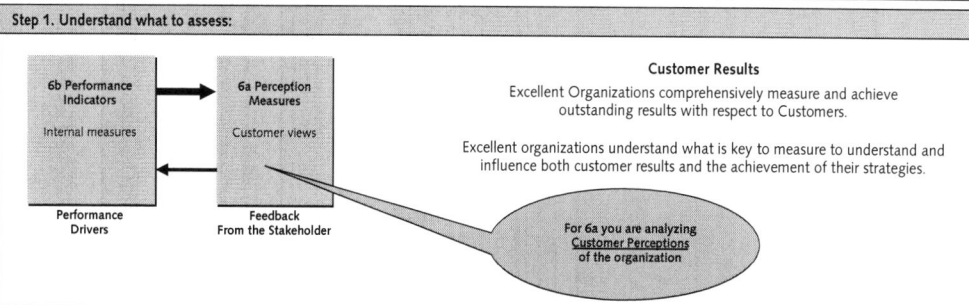

Step 2. Learn from what leaders in excellent organizations do for 6a:

From a measurement/analysis perspective they are able to:

i. Identify the distinctive features of the particular markets they serve and the products or services they offer, and then ensure that **customer satisfaction is measured** appropriately in all of these areas
ii. **Understand the causes of trends**, over time, in key customer satisfaction results and market share gains/losses
iii. **Compare their customer performance to their targets** and understand/act upon the reasons for successes and shortfalls
iv. Understand what is likely to **drive/enable future customer loyalty** and satisfaction
v. **Segment customer satisfaction data** by customer and sector, to ensure that insights, resources, organization and improvement activity are appropriately targeted
vi. Compare their **performance to that of competitors** and/or 'best in class' organizations

From an **achievement perspective** they are able to demonstrate outstanding performance as indicated by:

vii. **Positive trends** on most/many of the key measures
viii. **Achievement of target** on most/many of the key measures
ix. **Favourable comparisons with competitors**/world class organizations in the key results
x. Confidence that the **results are likely to be sustained**

APPENDIX 1: A SET OF X32 ANALYSIS PRO-FORMA'S

Steps 3 -7 Create a Measure-Achievement Analysis for this Criterion-Part				
3: List key Data/Measures you use	4: Analyze Performance Trends (+/0/-)	5: Record Duration of Trends (yrs)	6: Comparison with your Targets (+/0/-)	7: Judge Comparison with others (+/0/-)

Step 8: List any Measures-Achievements that you perceive as key, but are missing

Step 9: Conclude an analysis of your key strengths and areas for improvement for this Criterion-Part

Strengths:	Areas for Improvement:

Step 10: Score your Analysis

Results Total:	%	Scope:	% :	Overall:	% :

Step 11: Tick one of the options to rank the strategic importance of addressing the issues arising from the analysis above

☐ Not relevant	☐ Useful	☐ Important	☐ Critical to our success

Customer Results — 6b

Step 1. Understand what to assess:

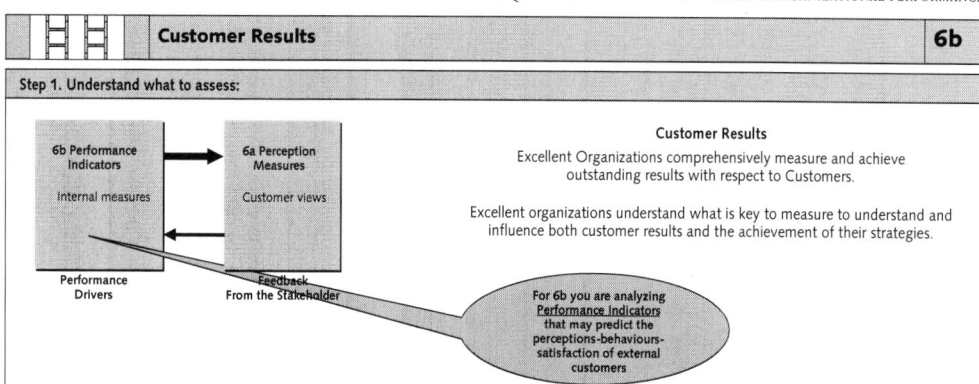

6b Performance Indicators — Internal measures → **6a Perception Measures** — Customer views

Performance Drivers / Feedback From the Stakeholder

Customer Results
Excellent Organizations comprehensively measure and achieve outstanding results with respect to Customers.

Excellent organizations understand what is key to measure to understand and influence both customer results and the achievement of their strategies.

For 6b you are analyzing Performance Indicators that may predict the perceptions-behaviours-satisfaction of external customers

Step 2. Learn from what leaders in excellent organizations do for 6b:

From a **measurement/analysis perspective** they are able to:

i. Identify a range of (typically) *internal* measures that are able to show performance trends with the internal activity thought likely to **enable/predict external customer satisfaction** (eg dependant on the organization improvement of end-to-end problem resolution time, increased innovation with known to be desirable product features, etc.)
ii. **Understand the causes of trends**, over time, in these results
iii. **Compare these results to targets** and understand/act upon the reasons for successes and shortfalls
iv. **Segment the data** by customer and sector, to ensure that insights, resources, organization and improvement activity are appropriately targeted
v. Compare their **performance to that of competitors** and/or 'best in class' organizations

From an **achievement perspective** they are able to demonstrate outstanding performance as indicated by:

vi. **Positive trends** on most/many of the key measures
vii. **Achievement of target** on most/many of the most important measures
viii. **Favourable comparisons with competitors**/world class organizations in the most important results
ix. Confidence that the **results are likely to be sustained**

APPENDIX 1: A SET OF X32 ANALYSIS PRO-FORMA'S

Steps 3-7 Create a Measure-Achievement Analysis for this Criterion-Part					
3: List key Data/Measures you use	4: Analyze Performance Trends (+/0/-)	5: Record Duration of Trends (yrs)	6: Comparison with your Targets (+/0/-)	7: Judge Comparison with others (+/0/-)

Step 8: List any Measures-Achievements that you perceive as key, but are missing

Step 9: Conclude an analysis of your key strengths and areas for improvement for this Criterion-Part	
Strengths:	Areas for Improvement:

Step 10: Score your Analysis					
Results Total:	%	Scope:	%:	Overall:	%:
Step 11: Tick one of the options to rank the strategic importance of addressing the issues arising from the analysis above					
☐ Not relevant	☐ Useful		☐ Important		☐ Critical to our success

People Results | 7a

Step 1. Understand what to assess:

- **7b Performance Indicators** — predictors measures — Performance Drivers
- **7a Perception Measures** — Customer views — Feedback From the Stakeholder

People Results

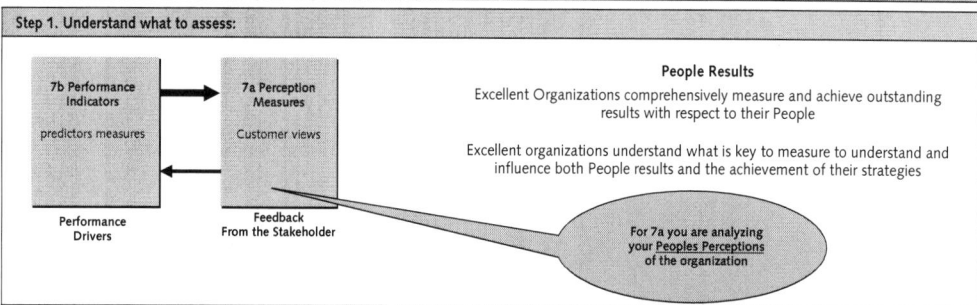

Excellent Organizations comprehensively measure and achieve outstanding results with respect to their People

Excellent organizations understand what is key to measure to understand and influence both People results and the achievement of their strategies

For 7a you are analyzing your Peoples Perceptions of the organization

Step 2. Learn from what leaders in excellent organizations do for 7a:

From a **measurement/analysis** perspective they are able to:

i. Identify the **most important drivers** of people satisfaction, commitment and motivation and then ensure that **people satisfaction is measured** appropriately in all of these areas
ii. **Understand the causes of trends**, over time, in key people results
iii. **Compare their people performance to their targets** and understand/act upon the reasons for successes and shortfalls
iv. Compare their **performance to that of others**/ 'best in class' organizations
v. **Segment the analysis of people data** by organizational units/level/sectors, to ensure that insights, resources, and improvement activity are appropriately targeted

From an **achievement perspective** they will be able to demonstrate outstanding performance as indicated by:

vi. **Positive trends** on most/many of the key measures
vii. **Achievement of target** on most/many of the key measures
viii. **Favourable comparisons with others**/world class organizations in the key results
ix. Confidence that the **results are likely to be sustained**

APPENDIX 1: A SET OF X32 ANALYSIS PRO-FORMA'S

Steps 3-7 Create a Measure-Achievement Analysis for this Criterion-Part				
3: List key Data/Measures you use	4: Analyze Performance Trends (+/0/-)	5: Record Duration of Trends (yrs)	6: Comparison with your Targets (+/0/-)	7: Judge Comparison with others (+/0/-)

Step 8: List any Measures-Achievements that you perceive as key, but are missing

Step 9: Conclude an analysis of your key strengths and areas for improvement for this Criterion-Part	
Strengths:	Areas for Improvement:

Step 10: Score your Analysis					
Results Total:	%	Scope:	%:	Overall:	%:
Step 11: Tick one of the options to rank the strategic importance of addressing the issues arising from the analysis above					
☐ Not relevant	☐ Useful		☐ Important		☐ Critical to our success

People Results — 7b

Step 1. Understand what to assess:

7b Performance Indicators — predictor measures — Performance Drivers

7a Perception Measures — Customer views — Feedback From the Stakeholder

People Results
Excellent Organizations comprehensively measure and achieve outstanding results with respect to their People

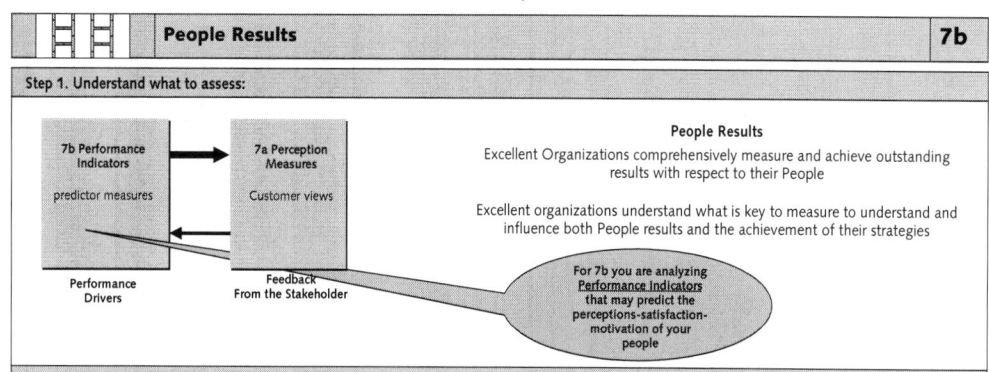

Excellent organizations understand what is key to measure to understand and influence both People results and the achievement of their strategies

For 7b you are analyzing Performance Indicators that may predict the perceptions-satisfaction-motivation of your people

Step 2. Learn from what leaders in excellent organizations do for 7b:

From a **measurement/analysis perspective** they are able to:

i. Identify a range of measures that are able to show performance trends with the activity thought likely to **enable/predict People satisfaction and motivation** (depending on the purpose of the organization, performance indicators for people may include results such as: success of training and development to meet objectives, involvement in improvement teams and suggestion schemes, accident, absenteeism and sickness levels, grievances and strikes, staff turnover and recruitment trends)
ii. **Understand the causes of trends**, over time, in these results
iii. **Compare these results to targets** and understand/act upon the reasons for successes and shortfalls
iv. **Segment the data** by organizational units/level/sectors, to ensure that insights, resources, and improvement activity are appropriately targeted
v. Compare their **performance to that of others** and/or 'best in class' organizations

From an **achievement perspective** they are able to demonstrate outstanding performance as indicated by:

vi. **Positive trends** on most/many of the key measures
vii. **Achievement of target** on most/many of the key measures
viii. **Favourable comparisons with others**/world class organizations in the key results
ix. Confidence that the **results are likely to be sustained**

APPENDIX 1: A SET OF X32 ANALYSIS PRO-FORMA'S

Steps 3-7 Create a Measure-Achievement Analysis for this Criterion-Part				
3: List key Data/Measures you use	4: Analyze Performance Trends (+/0/-)	5: Record Duration of Trends (yrs)	6: Comparison with your Targets (+/0/-)	7: Judge Comparison with others (+/0/-)

Step 8: List any Measures-Achievements that you perceive as key, but are missing

Step 9: Conclude an analysis of your key strengths and areas for improvement for this Criterion-Part	
Strengths:	Areas for Improvement:

Step 10: Score your Analysis					
Results Total:	%	Scope:	%:	Overall:	%:
Step 11: Tick one of the options to rank the strategic importance of addressing the issues arising from the analysis above					
☐ Not relevant	☐ Useful		☐ Important	☐ Critical to our success	

Society Results — 8a

Step 1. Understand what to assess:

Society Results

Excellent Organizations comprehensively measure and achieve outstanding results with respect to Society.

Excellent organizations understand what is key to measure to understand and influence both Society results and the achievement of their strategies

Diagram: 8b Performance Indicators (Internal measures / Performance) ↔ 8a Perception Measures (Society's views / Feedback)

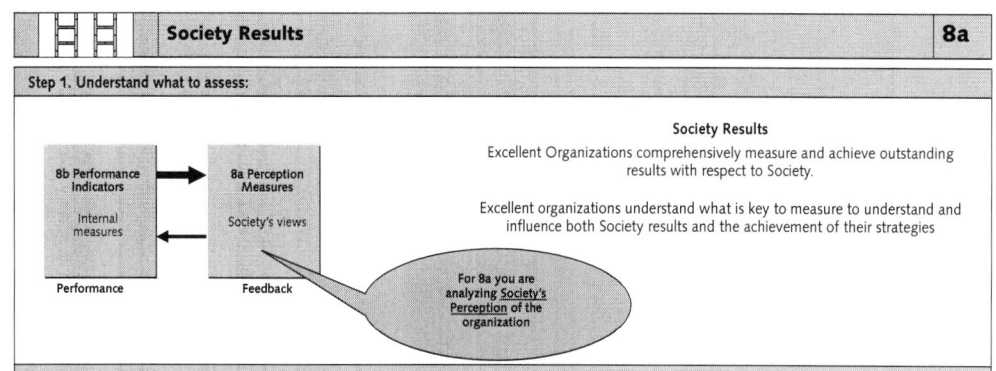

For 8a you are analyzing Society's Perception of the organization

Step 2. Learn from what leaders in excellent organizations do for 8a:

From a **measurement/analysis perspective** they are able to:

i. Identify a **range of societal perception measures** which will provide insights as to how their organization is perceived in the societies it operates in or impacts upon
ii. **Measure and track** these societal perceptions
iii. **Understand the causes of trends,** over time, in the results
iv. **Compare their organizations societal performance to targets** and understand/act upon the reasons for successes and shortfalls
v. Compare their **performance to that of others**/ 'best in class' organizations
vi. **Segment the analysis of societal data** by local, regional, national or global dimensions, as appropriate to the operations/products/services involved

From an **achievement perspective** they will be able to demonstrate outstanding performance as indicated by:

vii. **Positive trends** on most/many of the key measures
viii. **Achievement of target** on most/many of the key measures
ix. **Favourable comparisons with others** in the key results
x. Confidence that the **results are likely to be sustained**

Steps 3-7 Create a Measure-Achievement Analysis for this Criterion-Part

3: List key Data/Measures you use	4: Analyze Performance Trends (+/0/-)	5: Record Duration of Trends (yrs)	6: Comparison with your Targets (+/0/-)	7: Judge Comparison with others (+/0/-)

Step 8: List any Measures-Achievements that you perceive as key, but are missing

Step 9: Conclude an analysis of your key strengths and areas for improvement for this Criterion-Part

Strengths:	Areas for Improvement:

Step 10: Score your Analysis

Results Total:	%	Scope:	%:	Overall:	%:

Step 11: Tick one of the options to rank the strategic importance of addressing the issues arising from the analysis above

☐ Not relevant	☐ Useful	☐ Important	☐ Critical to our success

Society Results — 8b

Step 1. Understand what to assess:

Society Results

Excellent Organizations comprehensively measure and achieve outstanding results with respect to Society.

Excellent organizations understand what is key to measure to understand and influence both Society results and the achievement of their strategies

8b Performance Indicators — Internal measures — Performance
8a Perception Measures — Society's views — Feedback

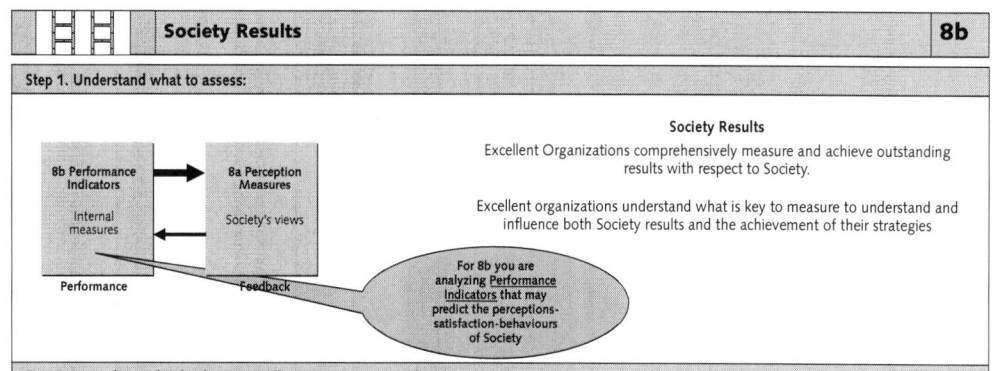

For 8b you are analyzing **Performance Indicators** that may predict the perceptions-satisfaction-behaviours of Society

Step 2. Learn from what leaders in excellent organizations do for 8b:

From a **measurement/analysis perspective** they are able to:

i. Identify a range of measures that are able to show performance trends with the activity thought likely to **enable/predict Societal perceptions of the organization** ((depending on the purpose of the organization, performance indictors for society may include examples such as: -levels of active involvement in community support, participation in community events, involvement in education and training, volunteering, environmental and ecological improvement activity, -Internal measures of trends in activities to reduce and prevent nuisance and harm to neighbours as a result of operations –levels of activities to assist the preservation of global resources such as energy, material resources, conservation, use of recycled material, reduction of waste, recycling, environmental and ecological impact issues)

ii. **Understand the causes of trends,** over time, in these results

iii. **Compare these results to targets** and understand/act upon the reasons for successes and shortfalls

iv. **Segment the analysis of this data** by local, regional, national or global dimensions, as appropriate to the operations/products/services involved

v. Compare their **performance to that of others** and/or 'best in class' organizations

From an **achievement perspective** they are able to demonstrate outstanding performance as indicated by:

vi. **Positive trends** on most/many of the key measures
vii. **Achievement of target** on most/many of the key measures
viii. **Favourable comparisons with others**/world class organizations in the key results
ix. Confidence that the **results are likely to be sustained**

APPENDIX 1: A SET OF X32 ANALYSIS PRO-FORMA'S

Steps 3-7 Create a Measure-Achievement Analysis for this Criterion-Part				
3: List key Data/Measures you use	4: Analyze Performance Trends (+/0/-)	5: Record Duration of Trends (yrs)	6: Comparison with your Targets (+/0/-)	7: Judge Comparison with others (+/0/-)

Step 8: List any Measures-Achievements that you perceive as key, but are missing

Step 9: Conclude an analysis of your key strengths and areas for improvement for this Criterion-Part

Strengths:	Areas for Improvement:

Step 10: Score your Analysis

Results Total:	%	Scope:	%:	Overall:	%:

Step 11: Tick one of the options to rank the strategic importance of addressing the issues arising from the analysis above

☐ Not relevant	☐ Useful	☐ Important	☐ Critical to our success

Key Performance Results — 9a

Step 1. Understand what to assess:

Key Performance Results

Excellent Organizations comprehensively measure and achieve outstanding results with respect to the key aspects of their Policy and Strategy.

For 9a you are analyzing your **Key Performance Outcomes**; those measures are your key results as defined in your Policy and Strategy

(Diagram: Criterion 2 Policy & Strategy, Criterion 4 Partnerships & Resources, Criterion 5 Processes → Key Enablers → 9b Key Performance / Internal measures (Predictors) → 9a Key Performance Outcomes / Outcome measures (Achievement to Plan))

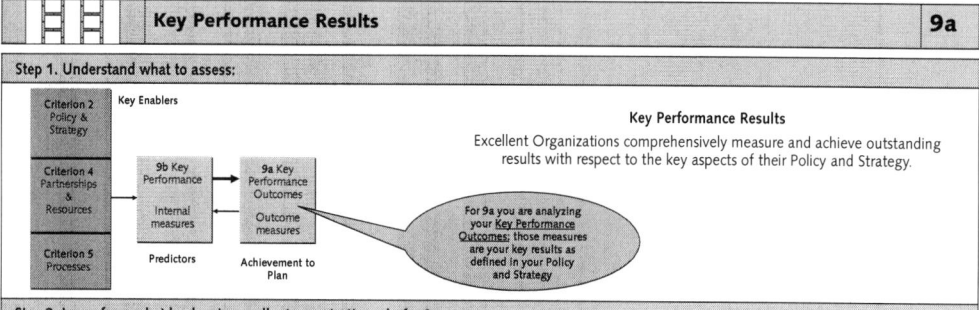

Step 2. Learn from what leaders in excellent organizations do for 9a:

From a **measurement/analysis perspective** they are able to:

i. Define and agree with key stakeholders **relevant financial measures** that will track the deployment/achievement of their chosen strategies. (these will typically include profit and loss, balance sheet, cash flow, and shareholder value-added in commercial organizations, and performance against budgets in non-commercial areas)

ii. Define a set of key **non-financial measures** that are indicative of success with the key strategic aims defined in the organization Policy and Strategy (depending on the type of organization and its strategy these may include measures such as market share, innovation rates, learning, breakthrough project activities, flexibility, and responsiveness to change)

iii. **Track and understand the causes of trends,** over time, in the results above

iv. **Compare their performance to their strategies, targets and plans,** on order to understand/act upon the reasons for successes and shortfalls

v. Understand what is likely to **drive/enable future success**

vi. **Segment their data** by organizational units/level/sectors, to ensure that insights, resources, and improvement activity are appropriately targeted;

vii. Compare their **performance to that of competitors** and/or 'best in class' organizations;

From an **achievement perspective** they will be able to demonstrate outstanding performance as indicated by:

viii. **Positive trends** on most/many of the key measures

ix. **Achievement of target** on most/many of the key measures

x. **Favourable comparisons with competitors**/world class organizations in the key results

xi. Confidence that the **results are likely to be sustained**

APPENDIX 1: A SET OF X32 ANALYSIS PRO-FORMA'S

Steps 3 -7 Create a Measure-Achievement Analysis for this Criterion-Part					
3: List key Data/Measures you use	4: Analyze Performance Trends (+/0/-)	5: Record Duration of Trends (yrs)	6: Comparison with your Targets (+/0/-)	7: Judge Comparison with others (+/0/-)

Step 8: List any Measures-Achievements that you perceive as key, but are missing

Step 9: Conclude an analysis of your key strengths and areas for improvement for this Criterion-Part	
Strengths:	Areas for Improvement:

Step 10: Score your Analysis						
Results Total:	%	Scope:	%:	Overall:		%:
Step 11: Tick one of the options to rank the strategic importance of addressing the issues arising from the analysis above						
☐ Not relevant		☐ Useful		☐ Important	☐ Critical to our success	

Key Performance Results — 9b

Step 1. Understand what to assess:

Key Performance Results
Excellent Organizations comprehensively measure and achieve outstanding results with respect to the key aspects of their Policy and Strategy.

For 9b you analyze your Key Performance Indicators. These measures are the operational ones used to monitor and understand the organizations processes and predict-improve the likely key performance outcomes

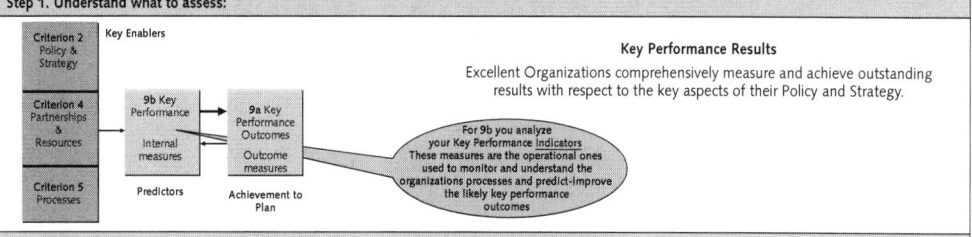

Step 2. Learn from what leaders in excellent organizations do for 9b:

From a measurement/analysis perspective they are able to:

i. Identify a range of measures that are able to show operational performance and help monitor, understand, predict and improve the organization's likely key performance outcomes in 9a (depending on the purpose and objectives of the organization and its processes, they may include those relating to (**Internal process measures** - performance and productivity, assessments, innovations and improvements, cycle times, defect rate, maturity and deployment, time to market: **External resources including partnerships** - supplier price and performance, number and value added of partnerships, number and value added of innovative products and services solutions generated by partners, number and value added of joint improvements with partners, recognition of partners' contribution: **Financial measures (those not reported in 9a)**- cash flow items, balance sheet items, depreciation and maintenance costs, return on net assets and equity, credit ratings: **Buildings, equipment and materials** - defect rates and shortages, inventory turnover, utility consumption, utilisation, service disruption: **Technology** - innovation rate, value of intellectual property, patents and royalties: **Information and knowledge** - integrity and accuracy, accessibility, relevance and timeliness, sharing and using knowledge and value of intellectual capital)

ii. **Understand the causes of trends,** over time, in these results

iii. **Compare these results to targets** and understand/act upon the reasons for successes and shortfalls

iv. **Segment the data** by organizational units/level/sectors, to ensure that insights, resources, and improvement activity are appropriately targeted;

v. Compare their **performance to that of others** and/or 'best in class' organizations;

From an achievement perspective they are able to demonstrate outstanding performance as indicated by:

vi. **Positive trends** on most/many of the key measures

vii. **Achievement of target** on most/many of the key measures

viii. **Favourable comparisons with others**/world class organizations in the key results

ix. Confidence that the **results are likely to be sustained**

APPENDIX 1: A SET OF X32 ANALYSIS PRO-FORMA'S

Steps 3-7 Create a Measure-Achievement Analysis for this Criterion-Part				
3: List key Data/Measures you use	4: Analyze Performance Trends (+/0/-)	5: Record Duration of Trends (yrs)	6: Comparison with your Targets (+/0/-)	7: Judge Comparison with others (+/0/-)

Step 8: List any Measures-Achievements that you perceive as key, but are missing

Step 9: Conclude an analysis of your key strengths and areas for improvement for this Criterion-Part

Strengths:	Areas for Improvement:

Step 10: Score your Analysis

Results Total:	%	Scope:	%:	Overall:	%:

Step 11: Tick one of the options to rank the strategic importance of addressing the issues arising from the analysis above

☐ Not relevant	☐ Useful	☐ Important	☐ Critical to our success

Appendix 2: Scoring Tools

An experienced and trained EFQM Assessor may use the EFQM tool known as RADAR; this involves assessing and scoring elements of **R**esults, **A**pproach, **D**eployment **A**ssessment and **R**eview.

Full understanding and confidence with the full RADAR approach typically only comes with extensive training (again more details at www.efqm.org see 'European Assessor Training' programs). In this book we propose the use of a simplified tool more able to be used by un-trained participants and without additional facilitation. However, before introducing this tool a little further understanding of RADAR maybe helpful.

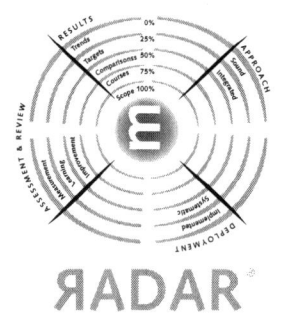

RADAR logic encourages an organization to be clear about the RESULTS it wants to achieve. It then analyzes whether an integrated set of sound ENABLERS designed to deliver these results exists.

In understanding RADAR scoring the first factor to be established is that for both '**enabler** criteria' and '**results** criteria' the scoring structure is multi-dimensional.

For enablers, assessors are looking at the performance in three dimensions, namely the 'nature of the **approach'**, the 'degree of **deployment'** that has been achieved and the '**assessment and review**' to determine effectiveness and improve.

Similarly, when looking at a results criterion assessors are looking at both the 'excellence of the **actual results achieved**', and at the '**scope**, or breadth of coverage of the results' presented.

Figure 7: The RADAR assessment process

Readers using the EFQM RADAR assessment process for the first time may be prepared to sacrifice a degree of scoring 'purity' and accuracy in exchange for a simpler and potentially more easily applied scoring system. The 'quick-score charts' on the following pages, coupled with their scoring summary sheet, provide just such a method. Alternatively, experienced readers may wish to use the full RADAR approach.

APPENDIX 2: SCORING TOOLS

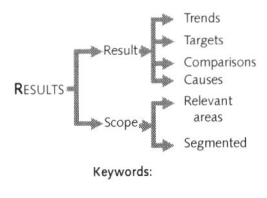

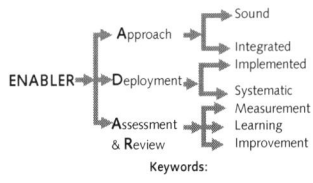

```
                    ┌─► Trends
           ┌─Result─┼─► Targets
           │        ├─► Comparisons
RESULTS ───┤        └─► Causes
           │        ┌─► Relevant areas
           └─Scope──┴─► Segmented
Keywords:
```

```
                    ┌─► Sound
           ┌─Approach──► Integrated
           │        └─► Implemented
ENABLER ───┼─Deployment──► Systematic
           │        ┌─► Measurement
           └─Assessment──► Learning
             & Review └─► Improvement
Keywords:
```

Figure 8: The RADAR assessment approach

Meaning of keywords:
Trends: These relate to positive movement of a result or sustained satisfactory or better performance over a period of time.
Targets: These relate to performance against a predetermined goal. The goal may be based on historical data, benchmarking, stakeholder need or other appropriate references.
Comparisons: We are now making a judgment as to what extent the results of the organization compares its performance to other reference points. As a minimum seeking comparisons with external organizations, competitor and industry averages. For role model organizations, comparisons with average will not be good enough - they will show comparisons with best-in-class organizations, within their own sector and with world-class as well.
Cause: The links to approaches that indicate how a leading position will be maintained.
Scope: A judgment as to the relevance of the measures presented within the business context of the organization being assessed and if they are appropriately segmented

Meaning of keywords:
Sound: The extent to which the approach has a clear rationale, defined processes and focuses on stakeholder needs.
Integrated: The extent to which the approach supports policy and strategy, and is linked to other approaches where appropriate.
Implemented: The extent to which the approach is implemented.
Systematic: The extent to which the deployment is carried out in a structured way with the method used to ensure deployment being itself planned and executed soundly.
Measurement: The extent to which regular and appropriate measurement of the effectiveness of the approach and deployment takes place.
Learning: The extent to which learning activities take place to identify best practices and improvement opportunities.
Improvement: The extent to which the output from measurement and learning is analyzed and used in order to identify, prioritise, plan and implement improvements.

'Quick-Score': Enablers

	Decision 1: Score the **Approaches** used for the criterion-part				
	Doing Nothing	Just Starting	Some relevant, soundly based approaches in place	Many proven relevant well integrated approaches	Role model approaches fully integrated into normal working practices
Score	0	4	8	12	16

Keep in mind that:
- **Soundly based:** means the approaches have clear rationales, defined processes and focus on stakeholder needs.
- **Integrated:** means that the approaches support policy and strategy and are linked to other approaches where appropriate.

	Decision 2: Score **Deployment** of the approaches above				
	Not Started	Implemented to less than 25% of full potential	Systematic execution to 50% of full potential	Systematic execution to 75% of full potential	Robustly deployed to full potential
Score	0	4	8	12	16

Keep in mind that:
- **Implemented:** means the extent to which the approach is put into effective use / deployment.
- **Systematic:** means that as well as being deployed you judge that the deployment was carried out in a structured way with the method used to ensure deployment being itself planned and executed soundly.

	Decision 3: Score **Assessment and Review** mechanisms				
	Non-existent	Occasional measurement	Evidence of measurement and some learning and improvement	Regular, effective measurement, learning and improvement	All approaches regularly reviewed, learning and improvements in place
Score	0	4	8	12	16

Keep in mind that:
- **Measurement:** means the extent to which regular and appropriate measurement of the effectiveness of the approach and deployment takes place.
- **Learning:** means the extent to which learning activities take place to identify best practices and improvement opportunities.
- **Improvement:** means the extent to which the output from measurement and learning is analyzed and used in order to identify, prioritise, plan and implement improvements.

APPENDIX 2: SCORING TOOLS

To use this method readers should:

- first complete an analysis of strengths and areas for improvement for each of the enabler criterion parts (in Appendix 1)
- then make the three 'scoring decisions' illustrated on the 'quick-score' charts
- transfer the score for each decision in the charts to the table below to obtain an approximate RADAR percentage score

Criteria	Decision 1 Score	Decision 2 Score	Decision 3 Score	Total Score (1+2+3)	X Factor	Predicted Overall %
1a					2.0	
1b					2.0	
1c					2.0	
1d					2.0	
1e					2.0	
2a					2.0	
2b					2.0	
2c					2.0	
2d					2.0	
3a					2.0	
3b					2.0	
3c					2.0	
3d					2.0	
3e					2.0	
4a					2.0	
4b					2.0	
4c					2.0	
4d					2.0	
4e					2.0	
5a					2.0	
5b					2.0	
5c					2.0	
5d					2.0	
5e					2.0	

Note: This process is perhaps most useful for quick initial assessments, where an early robustness in analysis of strengths and areas for improvement is more important than scoring precision

-Over time investment and training in using the full RADAR approach will usually bring benefit if a more robust scoring analysis is sought

'Quick-Score': Results

Decision 1: Scope-Relevance of Measures				
No relevant measurements	Few relevant measurements	Some to many measurements of relevant parameters	Regular measurements of most relevant parameters	Regular measurement of all relevant parameters
Score 0	6	10	14	18

Note: Relevant means proven to be of value to the appropriate stakeholder(s) of the Criterion being assessed.

Decision 2: Trends and Targets				
On balance, overall negative trends exist	Some positive trends and satisfactory comparisons with own targets	Positive trends over 3+ years and favourable comparisons with own targets on at least half of the results	Positive trends over 3+ years and favourable comparisons with own targets in at least 3/4 of the results	Strongly positive trends in all relevant results for 3+ years. Excellent comparisons against own targets
Score 0	4	8	12	16

Note: Trends should be demonstrable by *readily available* data sources.

Decision 3: Analysis of Results (Context and cause)				
No analysis	Analysis shows some results caused by own approach. Few external comparisons made or favourable	Several results clearly caused by own approach. Favourable external performance comparisons on at least half the results	Favourable comparisons with external organizations in most relevant areas. Most results caused by own effort	Excellent comparisons with competitors and/or best in class organizations Enabler cause and effect visible
Score 0	4	8	12	16

To use this method readers should:

- first complete an analysis of strengths and areas for improvement for each of the result criterion parts (in Appendix 1)
- then make the three 'scoring decisions' illustrated on the 'quick-score' charts
- transfer the score for each decision in the charts to the table below to obtain an approximate RADAR percentage score

Criteria	Decision 1 Score	Decision 2 Score	Decision 3 Score	Total Score (1+2+3)	X Factor	Predicted Overall %
6a					2.0	
6b					2.0	
7a					2.0	
7b					2.0	
8a					2.0	
8b					2.0	
9a					2.0	
9b					2.0	

Note: This process is perhaps most useful for quick initial assessments, where an early robustness in analysis of strengths and areas for improvement is more important than scoring precision. Over time investment and training in using the full RADAR approach will usually bring benefit if a more robust scoring analysis is sought.

Readers wishing to undertake <u>*EFQM Points Scoring comparisons*</u> should use the weighted tables below, transferring the criterion part <u>*percentage scores*</u> from the previous enabler and results score charts to this final table

1 Enabler averages

Criterion Number	1	%	2	%	3	%	4	%	5	%
Sub-Criterion	1a		2a		3a		4a		5a	
Sub-Criterion	1b		2b		3b		4b		5b	
Sub-Criterion	1c		2c		3c		4c		5c	
Sub-Criterion	1d		2d		3d		4d		5d	
Sub-Criterion	1e				3e		4e		5e	
Sum										
		÷ 5		÷ 4		÷ 5		÷ 5		÷ 5
Criterion Score awarded										

Note: The criterion score awarded is the arithmetic average of the overall % scores of the sub-criteria

2 Result weightings

Criterion Number	6	%		7	%		8	%		9	%	
Sub-Criterion	6a	x 0.75		7a	x 0.75		8a	x 0.25		9a	x 0.50	
Sub-Criterion	6b	x 0.25		7b	x 0.25		8b	x 0.75		9b	x 0.50	
Criterion core Awarded												

Note: The criterion score awarded is the total (a+b) of the weighted 'a' and 'b' % scores

3 Calculation of total weighted points (ie the final points/1000)

Criterion	Score Awarded	Factor	Points Awarded
1 Leadership		x 1.0	
2 Policy & Strategy		x 0.8	
3 People		x 0.9	
4 Partnerships and Resources		x 0.9	
5 Processes		x 1.4	
6 Customer Results		x 2.0	
7 People Results		x 0.9	
8 Society Results		x 0.6	
9 Key Performance Results		x 1.5	
Total Points Awarded			

My notes after completing the assessment above:

Appendix 3: Comparison Tables

104 Applicants in period 2004-06

One advantage of using RADAR or an EFQM calibrated scoring mechanism is that it enables organizations to compare their scores with those organizations applying to win the EFQM Excellence Award. The following tables show the points score achieved by all applicants in the period 2004-06 (on the y-axis) and the percentage number of applicants achieving each band (on the x-axis). So for example, looking at total point scores, only 3% of the total 104 applicants have ever achieved a 'Total' score of 751+ weighted overall points/1000 or above.

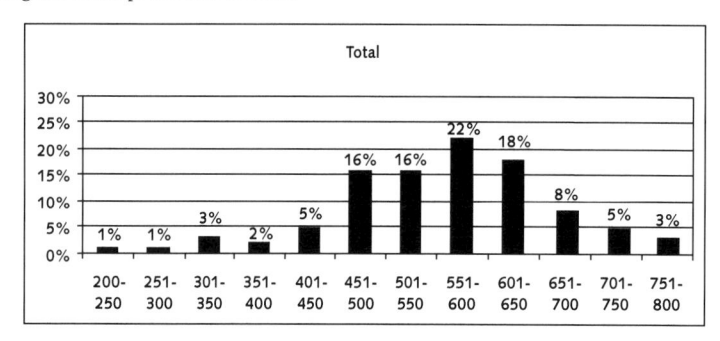

Total

Range	%
200-250	1%
251-300	1%
301-350	3%
351-400	2%
401-450	5%
451-500	16%
501-550	16%
551-600	22%
601-650	18%
651-700	8%
701-750	5%
751-800	3%

In leadership the Leadership criterion only 2% ever scored over an average of 80% (%= average of responses for each criterion part 1a through to 1e -that is 1a + 1b + 1c + 1d + 1e/5)

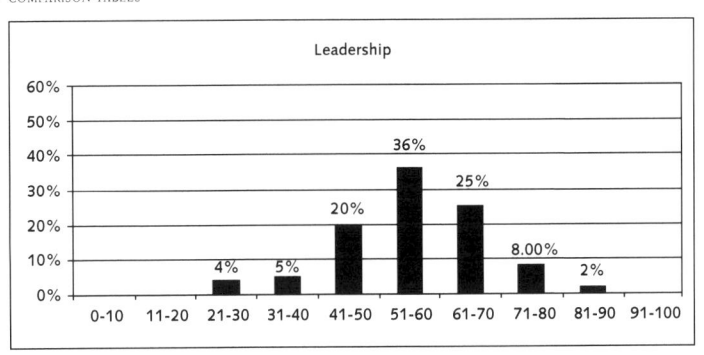

APPENDIX 3: COMPARISON TABLES

Leadership

Range	%
0-10	
11-20	
21-30	4%
31-40	5%
41-50	20%
51-60	36%
61-70	25%
71-80	8.00%
81-90	2%
91-100	

Without further comment the following tables show the averaged Criterion %'s attained by Applicants to the Award in Criteria 2 through to 9 in the period 2004-06

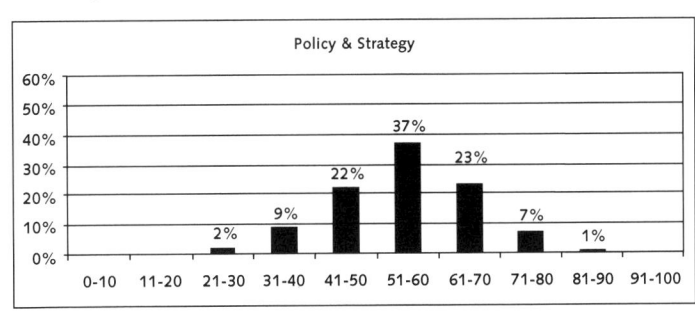

Policy & Strategy

Range	%
0-10	
11-20	
21-30	2%
31-40	9%
41-50	22%
51-60	37%
61-70	23%
71-80	7%
81-90	1%
91-100	

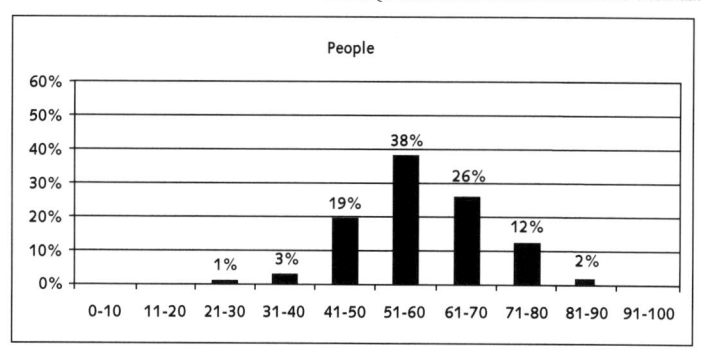

People

Range	%
0-10	
11-20	
21-30	1%
31-40	3%
41-50	19%
51-60	38%
61-70	26%
71-80	12%
81-90	2%
91-100	

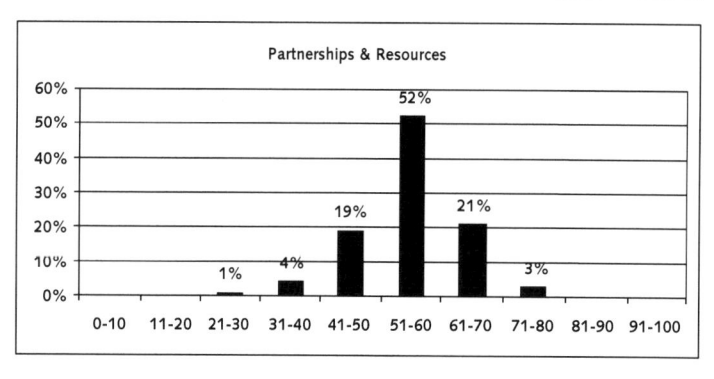

Partnerships & Resources

Range	%
0-10	
11-20	
21-30	1%
31-40	4%
41-50	19%
51-60	52%
61-70	21%
71-80	3%
81-90	
91-100	

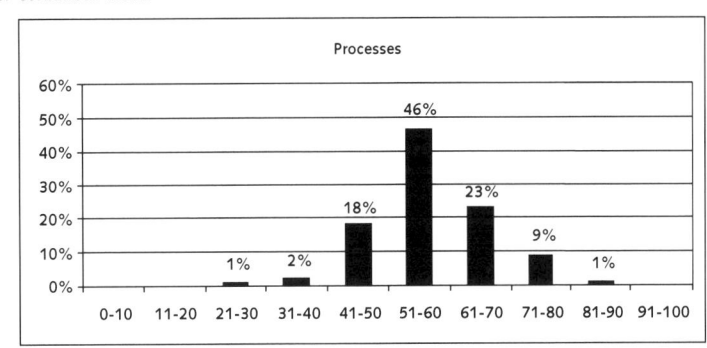

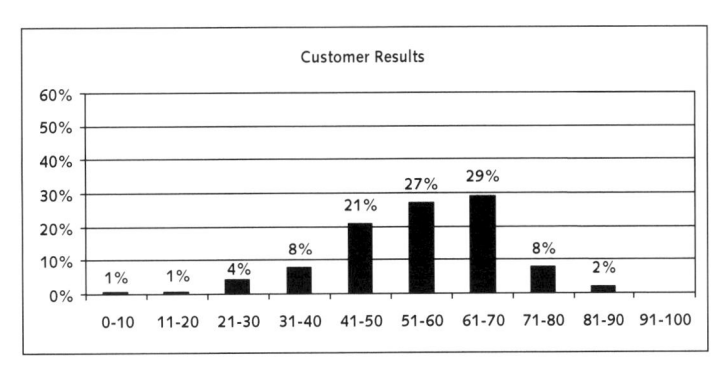

APPENDIX 3: COMPARISON TABLES

Processes

Range	Percentage
0-10	
11-20	
21-30	1%
31-40	2%
41-50	18%
51-60	46%
61-70	23%
71-80	9%
81-90	1%
91-100	

Customer Results

Range	Percentage
0-10	1%
11-20	1%
21-30	4%
31-40	8%
41-50	21%
51-60	27%
61-70	29%
71-80	8%
81-90	2%
91-100	

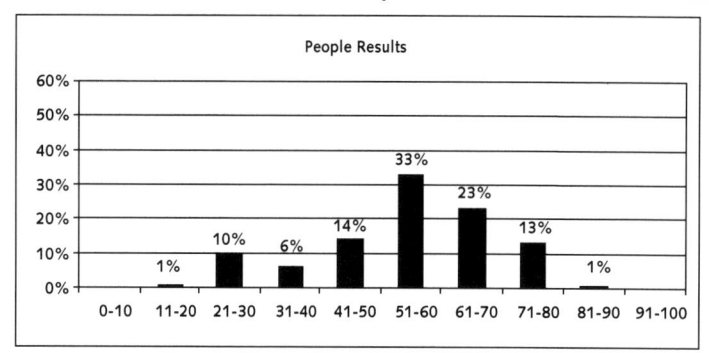

People Results

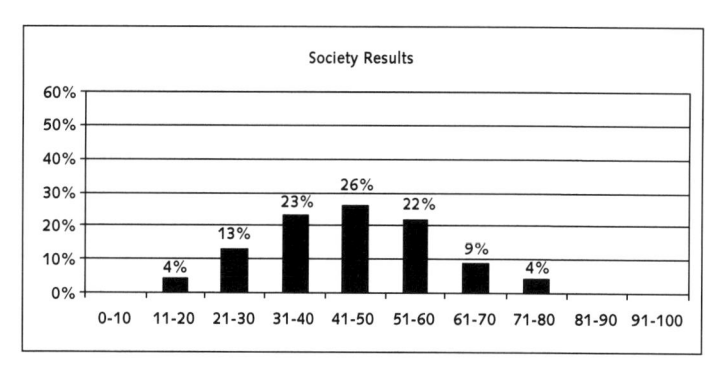

Range	Percentage
0-10	
11-20	1%
21-30	10%
31-40	6%
41-50	14%
51-60	33%
61-70	23%
71-80	13%
81-90	1%
91-100	

Society Results

Range	Percentage
0-10	
11-20	4%
21-30	13%
31-40	23%
41-50	26%
51-60	22%
61-70	9%
71-80	4%
81-90	
91-100	

APPENDIX 3: COMPARISON TABLES

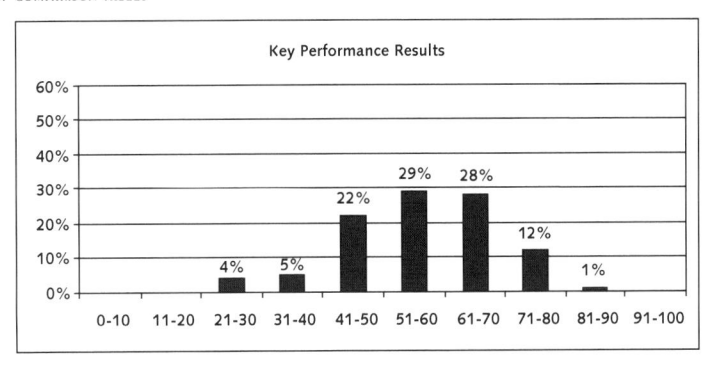

Key Performance Results

Range	Percentage
0-10	0%
11-20	0%
21-30	4%
31-40	5%
41-50	22%
51-60	29%
61-70	28%
71-80	12%
81-90	1%
91-100	0%

What conclusions can be drawn from this data?

The preceding nine tables will help to show you, in numerical terms, where you are on your journey towards excellence. You probably need to manage your own expectations carefully, as analysis of these tables will have shown you that those (104 Applicants for the European Excellence Award) who represent the upper decile of European organizations:

- have never scored more than 800 points out of the 1000 available; with this process, *50% is not average* and those scoring more than 500/1000 (ie 50%) are typically Award finalists or recognized organizations
- many of the 104 Applicant organizations score below 50% in some criteria

Knowing where you are and identifying the 'gap', in numerical terms, between yourself and others, can help you to prioritize your thoughts on what still needs to be done. It is suggested that you plot some simple bar chart profiles of your current successes and then target possible outcomes. However, it is also most important to review the related strengths and areas for improvement which have been generated in your analysis, and which lead to the numerical conclusion. The numbers are a by product of this technique; deriving and actioning the related analysis (see steps 4 and 5 of the five step process) is the key to success.

What characterizes some of the very best?

There is no prescription for Excellence; your review of the EFQM Award winner's good practices highlighted in Appendix 1 will have demonstrated this. However, analysis of some of the most successful organizations (those scoring in the 600-800 point bands) shows that some generic features/practices exist. So, as a final thought, here are some of the things that typically exist in a 600+ organization:
- ✓ leaders know what they expect and how they will realize it
- ✓ the value chain is optimized, stakeholders are 'engaged', feedback and follow-up is systematic and responsive
- ✓ future value chains are foreseen, innovation is evident
- ✓ speed is evident in the organization; cycle time is a key driver, rapid deployment can occur
- ✓ stakeholder requirements and expectations are understood, targeted and balanced in both enablers and results
- ✓ the organization and its stakeholders as a whole can answer these questions:
  - what are we passionate about?
  - what is our key economic driver?
  - what can/should we become 'best in the world' at?
- ✓ there is an integration and synergy among all parts and processes of the organization
- ✓ there is substantial evidence of ongoing success with 'Assessment and Review' including:
  - many cycles of improvement driven by measurement and learning
  - learning from both inside and outside the organization, and sharing of achievements and best practices
- ✓ and, of course, the results show favourable comparisons with 'top' organizations, not average organizations; they have strongly positive trends and achievement of targets

Printed in Great Britain
by Amazon